Praise for *Future Focused Leaders*

As Bill Ziegler and Dave Ramage note, "Learning is the goal." They relentlessly focus on that goal and demonstrate the ways in which school leaders can ensure that all students do, in fact, learn. Their work advances the equity agenda and contributes to the overall understanding about the ways in which school leaders can work smarter, not harder. I appreciated the examples in this book that can be used to inform the practices of school leaders everywhere.

Douglas Fisher,
Professor of Educational Leadership
San Diego State University
San Diego, CA

In my own work I have come to the conclusion that the best ideas go from practice to theory. If you believe this, as I do, *Future Focused Leaders* is for you. Ziegler and Ramage have provided us with lots of ideas, stories, and key takeaways from many practitioners who have succeeded. Be prepared to be a proactive consumer of the ideas in this book and you will be amply rewarded.

Michael Fullan,
Professor Emeritus
University of Toronto
Toronto, Canada

School leaders will find many one-stop ideas that will help them innovate their school in practical, inexpensive ways.

Virginia E. Kelsen,
Executive Director, Career Readiness
Chaffey Joint Union High School District
Ontario, CA

Future Focused Leaders touches on all the topics that are relevant to school leaders today. Bill Ziegler and Dave Ramage hit on those nagging obstacles we face as school leaders and provide real examples of school leaders who turned obstacles into opportunities to innovate and invigorate their students, staff, and community relationships. The solutions offered in this book are unique and replicable. . . . The book challenges the status quo and pushes the reader to look at obstacles as an opportunity to innovate.

Nancy Alvarez,
Assistant Principal
Herman Lawson Early Childhood School
McKinney, TX

This is School Leadership 101—a comprehensive view of current and evolving leadership practices in an era of shared leadership, social networking, and envisioning the future of public education.

David G. Daniels,
High School Principal
Susquehanna Valley High School
Conklin, NY

Are you looking for ideas on how to build a better school community where technology isn't an outlier but part of the core conversation? *Future Focused Leaders* is the book for you. Through practical stories from practicing K–12 leaders around the country, to their Relate, Innovate, and Invigorate framework, you will walk away with a plethora of ideas and actionable steps to get those ideas started.

Peter DeWitt,
Corwin Author/Consultant
Finding Common Ground blog (Education Week)
Albany, NY

Future Focused Leaders delivers on its promise to provoke a dialogue about meaningful change. Learn from leaders from every corner of the country and hear how they are innovating to meet the needs of all students. This is truly a book about a better tomorrow and how to get started today.

Brad Gustafson,
National Distinguished Principal and Author of Renegade Leadership
Greenwood Elementary School
Plymouth, MN

This project is a wonderful tool for a lead learner to develop skills for next-level impact. These practical and powerful examples from #educhampions are powerful, practical, and will make a difference for students and staff in your school.

Derek McCoy,
Principal
West Rowan Middle School
Salisbury, NC

The authors eloquently tell stories of educators in the trenches leading change and enhance them with innovative resources. This book contains nuggets of information that are attainable for all of us and will be a reference source for me when setting goals. Ziegler and Ramage have produced a must-read for all school leaders and a reflective tool for leading and managing change.

Bethany Hill,
Principal
Central Elementary School
Rancho Cucamonga, CA

The educational world is full of linear ideas, one-size-fits-all best practices, and data- driven theories that continue to persuade school leaders to create second-rate replicas from the past. Thankfully, *Future Focused Leaders* provides hope for students and leaders who are strong enough to rise up against traditional silos. It showcases a diverse group of leaders who thrive on practice over theory, while providing an abundance of strategies for others to follow to create schools of tomorrow.

Glenn Robbins,
Superintendent
Tabernacle Township School District
Tabernacle, NJ

Equity, sustainable change, innovation, and moving the deep-seated attitudes of a community—these are all matters of culture. These issues transcend a single classroom, and none of this can take hold without principal leadership. Our work is so important, and it's crucial that we get it right. This book provides practical inspiration for all future focused leaders.

Alan Tenreiro,
NASSP Principal of the Year 2016
Cumberland High School
Cumberland, RI

School and district administrators understand that the role of leadership has become more complex and changes rapidly in response to demands and expanding knowledge. A major role for school leaders is to harness the expertise in their schools to lead successful transformations. *Future Focused Leaders* provides perspective and ideas for implementation, as well as inspiration for any leader. If you're looking for a book that will help you leverage digital tools, jumpstart innovation, or design learning environments where creativity is encouraged and transforms learning, then look no further! Bill Ziegler and Dave Ramage have successfully curated ideas and examples that will get you on your way!

Tammy Gibbons,
Director of Professional Development and Information
Association of Wisconsin School Administrators
Madison, WI

Future Focused Leaders is a fantastic resource for administrators at all levels of school leadership. The success stories lend themselves to change that can be made immediately to help students, staff, and communities. The Relate, Innovate, and Invigorate framework is a wonderful model to enhance leadership capacity through activities that will move your school and district forward!

Joe Sanfelippo,
Superintendent
Fall Creek School District
Fall Creek, WI

Bill and Dave capture the essence of school leadership, bringing it to life through their voices and the dynamic, authentic actions of school leaders across the nation. School leadership is about passion, people, and communication. They bring these qualities to the forefront with practical, and replicable, examples that make a difference in schools nationwide. Read this and prepare to "Relate, Innovate, and Invigorate." You will be the difference.

Michael E. Allison,
Principal
Hopewell High School
Aliquippa, PA

What a smorgasbord of greatness! Bill Ziegler and Dave Ramage will exceed your expectations in all they have poured into this book—including their hearts. They provide dynamic and realistic tips with real examples and tools. I've not seen a more inclusive book!

LaVonna Roth,
International Speaker/Consultant
Creator and Founder of Ignite Your S.H.I.N.E.®
Riverview, FL

Future Focused Leaders is a must- have for all leaders and aspiring leaders. Bill Ziegler and Dave Ramage frame their work in a way that makes it accessible to all readers. Not only do they provide ideas and share their thinking, but they also spotlight real-life examples of things happening in schools across our country today. They speak to the importance of communication in leadership and how that impacts relationships, engagement, and overall success of the community. This book serves as a guide of what could be when leaders make a dedicated and intentional effort to change things!

Tony Sinanis,
Author, Speaker, and Presenter
Plainedge Public Schools
Massapequa, NY

Future Focused Leaders

Future Focused Leaders

Relate, Innovate, and Invigorate for Real Educational Change

Bill Ziegler

Dave Ramage

Foreword by Salome Thomas-EL

CORWIN

A SAGE Publishing Company

FOR INFORMATION:

Corwin

A SAGE Company

2455 Teller Road

Thousand Oaks, California 91320

(800) 233-9936

www.corwin.com

SAGE Publications Ltd.

1 Oliver's Yard

55 City Road

London EC1Y 1SP

United Kingdom

SAGE Publications India Pvt. Ltd.

B 1/I 1 Mohan Cooperative Industrial Area

Mathura Road, New Delhi 110 044

India

SAGE Publications Asia-Pacific Pte. Ltd.

3 Church Street

#10-04 Samsung Hub

Singapore 049483

Executive Editor: Arnis Burvikovs

Senior Associate Editor: Desirée A. Bartlett

Editorial Assistant: Kaitlyn Irwin

Production Editor: Bennie Clark Allen

Copy Editor: Terri Lee Paulsen

Typesetter: C&M Digitals (P) Ltd.

Proofreader: Sue Schon

Indexer: Jeanne Busemeyer

Cover Designer: Anupama Krishnan

Marketing Manager: Nicole Franks

This book is printed on acid-free paper.

SFI Certified Sourcing
www.sfiprogram.org
SFI-00453

17 18 19 20 21 10 9 8 7 6 5 4 3 2 1

Contents

In addition to all of the resources you will find in this book, you will also be invited to participate in our interactive website to meet, share, and network with other school leaders. There you will find an authentic way to make our dialogue a two-way experience. The goal is to create a space where the conversation becomes relevant and timely long after the ink has dried on the pages of the text. Visit **www.chaselearning.org**.

Foreword

I always enjoy reading books that help school leaders improve their ability to change the culture in their schools and communities. As principal at a K–8 school in a high-needs community in Wilmington, Delaware, I am often the first in line for inspiration when authors or speakers offer information on developing relationships with our stakeholders, innovating in our schools, building community, and leveraging technology across all grades and supporting teachers with high-quality professional development. For too long educators and leaders have focused on what we have always done instead of what we need to do to impact the future for our students. Future focused leaders shatter the status quo. They build capacity in their schools and prepare their students and teachers for innovative changes that will challenge them to grow to new heights.

In this career and life-changing book, Bill Ziegler and Dave Ramage provide a plan for school leaders to not only embrace educational technology, but to incorporate it into every aspect of the lives of their students and staff. What makes *Future Focused Leaders* unique is the emphasis on the voices of school leaders and stories about the fantastic work happening around the country in our schools. I am a huge advocate of school principals and teachers promoting the positive culture and success in our schools and classrooms. Oftentimes the view from outside a school is much different than the perspective from the inside. In this age of social media, we need to master brand our schools. As educators, it is time we begin to brag outright about our schools and the wonderful things our teachers are accomplishing with our students. In addition, readers will learn how they can meet and network with school leaders and district administrators on an interactive website to engage in conversations around leadership. Now *that* is taking 21st century learning to another level!

I am recommending *Future Focused Leaders* to all school leaders who have a desire to learn more about building relationships, nurturing creativity in teachers and students, changing school culture, inspiring others to greatness and servant leadership. This book will quickly become a field manual for those on the front lines who want to be recognized as leaders who are making an impact on schools of the present and future. Bill and Dave have challenged us all to be better role models and leaders, and they have given us the tools to succeed on this very important mission. *Future Focused Leaders* will be on my desk next to my bible, and in the libraries of leaders around the world. I hope you will join the revolution to transform leadership and foster resiliency in our schools!

—Salome Thomas-EL (Principal EL),
Award-winning Principal, Author, and Speaker

Preface

We are writing this book with hopes of engaging in a dialogue with fellow school leaders and stirring them to a call to action. We want to use the resources in this book, our combined leadership experiences, your leadership stories, and untapped opportunities to relate, innovate, and invigorate our schools.

Much has been written about the promises and potholes surrounding educational technology. The rapidly changing world of digital learning seems to be calling us forward and yet backward simultaneously. The shift in technology has taken many leaders by surprise, not because they didn't see it coming, but because they underestimated its relevance.

We (the authors) would be considered early adopters. We do not move away from technology—we're more like moths to the flame! But even in our most successful moments of leading and extending learning with technology, we hear a voice calling us back to use technology for the greater good. We are reminded of a higher call.

School leaders have a unique responsibility to care for our greatest asset as a nation: our children. Families, faith communities, law enforcement, businesses, communities, nonprofits, agencies, and schools must work together to make a difference in the lives of our students. Because of this stewardship we cannot be mesmerized by the glitter of gadgets. We must connect with every student, show them a way into an unknown future, and celebrate our successes together along the way.

RELATE, INNOVATE, INVIGORATE

When schools miss the opportunity to know a student, invest in their life, and build a connection with them we become the worst example of a factory model. If we cannot *relate* to each other we are simply turning out isolated learners. At the 20-year reunion of this year's graduating class, alumni will not be talking about how you taught them their ABCs or how to solve a word problem, they will not be reciting the sonnets of Shakespeare or the

Preamble, and they probably will not be discussing logarithms before they toast to 20 sweet years. But, they will be reminiscing about the relationships shared with teachers, coaches, principals, and other staff members. These relationships, and the environment of trust built together, allow a learning organization to change and grow. Engaging an organization in new learning and thinking requires clear, consistent communication and trusting relationships to nurture a culture of innovation.

If we fail to model and teach innovation to our students we are destined to become a nation of followers who simply implement the powerful ideas of others. Arguably the one characteristic that sets us apart as Americans is our ability to *innovate*, yet if we are not careful caretakers of this legacy we will lose our defining trait. High-stakes testing, the elimination of art, music, and dance all nip at the heels of our innovative spirit. Let's use the power of technology to nurture and grow this vital, future focused skill.

We hope the chapters that follow will *invigorate* your work. There are plenty of political, financial, and societal complaints about schools. We don't turn away from our failures as an institution, but we recognize the need to celebrate our strengths. We celebrate the best that our collective practice has to offer—and highlight some of these practitioners in the pages that follow. Their success encourages and inspires us.

SPECIAL FEATURES

Future Focused Leaders has a structure that lets you read from start to finish, or jump in with a chapter that piques your curiosity.

- We start and end each chapter with a *School Leader's Story*. Including the voice of school leaders is a way to encourage all of us in the work. It's reassuring to learn how leaders are making a difference in the lives of their students, staff, and community.
- *Key Chapter Takeaways* appear near the end of each chapter and serve to focus ideas and inspire action. Remember, our desire is to have school leaders make a difference, not simply learn more stuff. We hope the chapters will get ideas flowing for your own leadership practice. This part of each chapter is designed to help move thinking into action where authentic learning can happen.
- *The Relate, Innovate, Invigorate* sections are designed to extend your learning. Practical ways to use the ideas from the chapter are organized in the three categories of Relate, Innovate, and Invigorate.
- Each chapter also includes an opportunity for your core leadership team to gather, engage in a *Team Talk* experience, and share your

results with other school leaders. These suggested tasks provide a practical, doable way to put ideas into practice. Share your experiences with other school leaders at **www.chaselearning.org/TeamTalk**.

- We hope you will be intrigued by the *Hyped-Up Front and Back Covers*. The front cover of this book and the author photograph on the back cover contain augmented reality messages for school leaders. In order to view these videos, follow these instructions:

  ○ Download the Aurasma app on your mobile device.

  ○ Open the Aurasma app. If you don't have an Aurasma account, create one.

  ○ Search for "Future Focused Leaders." When you see the campaign that includes the *Future Focused Leaders* book cover, select it and click "Follow."

  ○ On the Aurasma home screen, click the icon at the bottom center to open the viewfinder.

  ○ Point the Aurasma viewfinder at the front cover of Bill Ziegler's photo on the back cover and WOW! After a few seconds, the photo will transform into a video.

  ○ Caution - you need to be logged into your account for the app to work

  ○ To access the video, continue to hold the viewfinder over the image, if you move the viewfinder away, the video will stop playing.

- In addition to all of the resources you will find in this book, you will also be invited to participate in our *interactive website* to meet, share, and network with other school leaders. There you will find an authentic way to make our dialogue a two-way experience. The goal is to create a space where the conversation becomes relevant and timely long after the ink has dried on the pages of the text. Visit **www.chaselearning.org**.

WHY THIS BOOK

We believe this book offers school leaders a distinct and unique experience for leadership learning. After reading this book, you will gain insights, tips, and tools on how to

- strengthen your school culture by building deeper relationships through more meaningful conversations,
- effectively leverage digital tools to improve your school brand and build community partnerships,

- pursue partnerships to improve student learning,
- jumpstart innovation because the future is now,
- design learning environments where students thrive as creative innovators,
- leverage the unique strengths of your team to transform school culture,
- recall the reasons you entered into the education profession by re-examining the call to be a servant leader, and
- become a learning leader—one who is dedicated to personally learning every day.

We listen, create, fail, learn from mistakes, move ahead, and keep that cycle going for the sake of our students, staff, and community. We press on because we know it's our collective future that's at stake. Not knowing what the future workplace looks like is part of the challenge, but it's also energizing. We can provide skills and experiences that equip our students to thrive in the unknown future. One thing is certain: We cannot fail our children. If we lead to the future together, we will serve our students well.

"Technology has transformed our lives but not our learning. We have a responsibility, as school leaders, to use technology to engage, equip, and inspire students to change our world for good."

Acknowledgments

I want to thank my parents, Bill and Linda Ziegler, who raised me to always have a curious mind, to show kindness to others, and to give my best in all that I do. Their love blesses me beyond measure. To my sister, Jane, thank you for teaching me about life's beautiful blessings; I will forever live out your legacy. Philippians 4:13.

I am grateful for the love and support of my wife, Kim, and our two children, David and Hannah; you inspire me each day to press on, work hard, and to dream big!

Bill Ziegler, EdD

I want to thank my first educational leaders, my mom and dad. You both modeled lifelong learning (still do) and helped me find the joy in reading, questioning, creating, and learning. You made sure I learned all my kindergarten lessons well.

There's no way I could accomplish the work of writing, or leading, without the support of my wife, Diane, and our children, Matthew, Laura, and Emily. Each of you is an inspiration to me, and I'm truly blessed to have you in my life. We press on together, striving for what lies ahead—always more to learn.

Dave Ramage, PhD

Special thanks to Arnis Burvikovs and Desirée Bartlett at Corwin Press for their leadership and expertise. We would like to also thank the Corwin team of Kaitlyn Irwin, Bennie Clark Allen, Terri Lee Paulsen, Anupama Krishna, and Nicole Franks, and our peer reviewers.

We also want to thank the many educators and leaders who helped guide our thinking and our leadership practices. Not all can be named, but each interaction has helped shape us to be the people we are today. Thanks to all the school leaders working diligently to make a difference for your students and your community.

About the Authors

Bill Ziegler is a high school principal in Pennsylvania. He was recently honored as the 2016 Pennsylvania Principal of the Year, the 2015 National Association of Secondary School Principals Digital Award winner, and was selected to serve on the United States team of school leaders to the Great Leaders Summit in China. Dr. Ziegler has more than 24 years of service in public education where he served as a school leader for 20 years. He has served as a high school social studies teacher, high school assistant principal, middle school principal, and he currently serves as a high school principal. He also earned Apple Teacher certification and was recently selected to participate in an Apple Research Study for School Leaders. He is honored to be part of the Corwin Consulting Team that provides high-quality professional development to school leaders. Dr. Ziegler also serves as an adjunct professor at Temple University in their Masters of Education department. He is very active in his state; he served as the president of the Pennsylvania Principals Association in 2014 and 2016, and was honored to be selected as treasurer and southeast regional representative for the same association. Dr. Ziegler presents regularly around the world on school leadership. He has presented at national conferences such as the National Association of Secondary School Principals, Association of Curriculum and Supervision Development, International Society for Technology in Education, and many more. He spoke on Capitol Hill to lobby for better E-rate coverage for schools throughout the United States. Dr. Ziegler also hosts a nationally syndicated radio program called "TIPPS" (Teachers in Public/Private Schools), where he provides tips for students, parents, and educators on education. He also volunteers with Christian Educators Association International. Dr. Ziegler is the owner of Chase Learning (https://chaselearning.org), a private educational consulting firm designed to provide high-quality and engaging professional development to strengthen school leaders throughout the United States.

Personally, he is married to his beautiful wife, Kim, and they have two high school aged children. He can often be found fly fishing in the streams of Pennsylvania, cheering on his favorite Philly sports teams, or playing his saxophone in church.

Contact:

Twitter: @drbillziegler
Voxer: drbillziegler
E-mail: drbillziegler@gmail.com
Website: https://chaselearning.org

 **Dave Ramage** is a practicing school leader serving as a middle school principal in Pennsylvania. He has served in the public school system for 30 years as a music teacher, K–12 instructional coach, coordinator of technology staff development, director of education, assistant principal, and his current role as middle school principal. Dr. Ramage earned his PhD in educational leadership and technology learning from Drexel University, where he serves as a member of the adjunct faculty. He is blessed to be married to his bride, Diane, for 30 years. They have three children. He is an avid bass player and loves to spend summer vacation time at the beach with his family.

Conversational Leadership

Leadership Driven by Relationships, Listening, and Communication

"The conversation is the relationship."

—Ray Jorgensen

*T*his chapter helps leaders understand the power of relationships to drive organizations and produce sustainable change. Perhaps the single strongest indicator of the health of an organization is the quality of the relationships within that organization. We will give practical strategies that leverage the power of conversation to strengthen existing relationships and forge new ones. The primary focus will be the relationships between school leader and professional staff, but the principles will also be applied to students, parents/guardians, and community stakeholders. We will discuss how a positive school culture leads to student engagement and connectedness. The chapter will end with a simulation that is best to be completed by your team of school leaders. This simulation will challenge school leaders to examine a difficult teacher situation and respond accordingly. The simulation is titled *The Bully Teacher.*

	School Leader's Story
	Listening to Student Voice

Leader:	Brian Pickering (2016 New Hampshire Principal of the Year)
School:	Contoocook Valley Regional High School

(Continued)

(Continued)

Website: http://cvhs.convalsd.net/

Setting: Rural

Size: 759 students

Grades: 9–12

Population: 95% white, 2% Asian, 2% multiracial, 1% African American

Poverty: 27.9% economically disadvantaged

District: Contoocook Valley Regional School District, SAU#1

Location: Peterborough, NH

Photo courtesy of Brian Pickering

In his first year as principal at Contoocook Valley (ConVal) Regional High School, a student asked Brian Pickering if she could get extra help from her physics teacher during advisory. She couldn't see her teacher at any other time outside of class—not during lunch because she and her teacher were assigned different lunch periods, not before school because she depended on the school bus for transportation, and not after school because she played a sport and the team was heading to the playoffs. When Pickering looked at the school schedule, he realized that, even with an advisory system, there simply was no time in the day for the student to get the help she needed.

What followed was a year-long process of out-of-the-box thinking and experimentation by an interdisciplinary group of dedicated teachers, staff, and school counselors. After conducting surveys and holding focus group sessions with students and parents, Teachers in Academic Support Centers (TASC) was inaugurated at ConVal High School in the fall of 2011.

"When we first created TASC, our primary goal was to meet the varying needs of our 700-plus student population. We wanted to make sure that students could find time for relearning opportunities, take advantage of enrichment and extension activities, and could access social and emotional supports at a dedicated time during the school day," Pickering said.

At ConVal, TASC is now an important part of the daily routine. ConVal runs on a four by four block schedule, and TASC is a half-block of flexible time in the middle of the school day. On Mondays, groups of about 15 students meet with their homeroom mentors to determine their schedules for the week. Schedules change from week to week. "A big part of TASC is students taking responsibility for their own learning," Pickering explained. "Students have a choice to engage in enrichment activities and extensions of their learning, as long as they are performing well academically."

When student performance slips, classroom teachers and homeroom mentors take over and assign students to academic interventions where they can make up a skills deficit. Homework, too, can be completed during TASC, frequently in consultation with the student's classroom teacher who can re-explain an important concept that a student may have missed in class. TASC interventions have vastly reduced the time interval between the development of a learning deficit and addressing that shortcoming. According to student surveys, on average about two TASC interventions are sufficient to bring them back up to speed. TASC has resulted in improved student learning and bolstered student agency in the learning process.

As a secondary benefit, disciplinary issues have sharply decreased. "We have noticed an over 50% reduction in disciplinary cases in the last five years. Can we attribute all of that to TASC alone? Probably not," Pickering said. "But with the firm connection to their homeroom mentors and the varied interactions between students and teachers in small groups, we believe that TASC has been a strong contributing factor to this improvement because of increased student engagement."

Other schools have taken notice of the ConVal model and introduced their own versions of TASC—iTime, the Bear Block, and PAWS, to name just a few. In all, over 100 schools in New England and some as far away as Georgia, Texas, Colorado, and California have instituted their own flexible time schedule based on ConVal's example.

"We never expected that what we were creating five years ago would make such a difference, for so many schools and so many students," Pickering said. "It is a powerful testimony to our belief, as a school, that being attentive to the needs of any individual student can have wide-ranging, positive outcomes for all."

If you view the TASC example as merely innovative scheduling you missed the most powerful change—how it fortified relationships between students and staff. We believe relationship building is the number one skill needed to be a strong school leader. It's all about relationships! Relationships are at the core of what we do as school leaders. Without the ability to build positive, caring, and sustaining relationships, school leaders will struggle in their daily and long-term work.

Relationships are all about what we do; relationships are the heartbeat of a school leader's life. Our relationships connect us to our school community or pull us away from the people that make the greatest difference in the school. When our relationships are healthy, everything else is so much easier. Relating is about knowing people, trusting people, and caring for them. If you want to lead your people, you must know them and love them.

The importance of relationships as school leaders is so key in moving a school culture forward. If relationships, at any level, are not functioning at their best, the school culture suffers and growth is hampered. The simulation at the end of this chapter will walk school leaders through a realistic and difficult interaction with a teacher that is impacting the school's culture. As the school leader, you will be asked to make decisions on how you would resolve the issue. We encourage you to complete the simulation with your team of school leaders and talk and reflect on your decision-making process.

THE CONVERSATION IS THE RELATIONSHIP

As a school leader, the ability to communicate is critical to the effectiveness of your leadership. To communicate in a caring, relational, and positive way is necessary to thrive as a school leader. Relationships are built on conversations, and in this segment we will share key ways to strengthen your conversations. We discuss how to strengthen your communication skills, how to speak from the heart, how to suspend certainty, hold space for difference, and work to slow down the conversation. This work around relationships and conversations will strengthen how you lead faculty meetings, small groups, and learning conversations with teachers.

I learned everything in this chapter from my good friend, my principal coach, and leadership expert, Ray Jorgensen of Jorgensen Learning Center (Jorgensen & Hurst, 2009). Jorgensen's work in my life has enriched me to be a stronger school leader who is committed to building relationships and learning through conversations. He likes to remind his clients that, "the conversation *is* the relationship." This is not an either–or situation. If we are going to relate and work together we must learn to talk and listen to one another well.

Listen for Understanding

First, let's take a look at listening for understanding. I know you are probably thinking, I got this skill, I'm a great listener. Well, before you skip over this section, I'd like you to consider a few key points about listening for understanding. When a school leader listens for understanding, they aren't just trying to hear what the person is saying, they are listening intently to understand what the person is sharing. When I started listening for understanding, I didn't just become a better school leader—I grew as a husband, father, and man.

Let's get the easy step out of the way: Rid yourself of distraction while listening to someone. Whether it be that cell phone buzzing with incoming texts, daydreaming, or simply being distracted by your surroundings, make sure that you focus on the person talking. Look them in the eye, nod and give body gestures that show you are listening, and reiterate what they are saying so you check for understanding.

Even after you've taken these steps and physically cleared a path for listening, you're not quite ready. For most of us the even-more difficult attention to focus is our mental attention. You can turn off the phone, close the laptop or tablet, look someone straight in the eye, and still have your own ideas and responses running through your head as they speak. The real discipline comes from truly hearing what they are saying. We'll talk about some skills to help you do this later in the chapter.

There is no greater way to demonstrate that you care for someone, value their contribution to the school community, and share their goals for success than by hearing them. When the conversation has ended the real gift you can give is to have the person walk away and know they've been heard. This is how conversation becomes the relationship. At the end of the chapter, you will have a unique opportunity to listen for understanding in a simulation; take time to complete the simulation and reflect on what you learned.

Checks for Understanding

Conversations can often be misunderstood. I'm sure we all participated in the Whisper Down the Lane or the Telephone Game as a kid. By the end of the line, the statement is so mixed up that it regularly has no similarity to what was originally spoken. Have you ever talked to a teacher or a student and they heard you say something very different from what you meant? This is why I will frequently restate what I heard the person I am listening to say. For instance, let's say a teacher stops you in the hallway to share how a student is causing them major frustration as the student constantly acts out in class. In this case, I'd probably say, "What I am hearing you say is that a certain student who is acting out is causing you frustration in your class, is that correct?" This is called a check for understanding. This one quick and easy strategy clears up so much misunderstanding you would be shocked. As we listen, we instantly filter what's being said and we frequently jump to conclusions. We will talk about suspending certainty later, but for this section it's key to complete a check for understanding. Below are some checks for understanding that you can use in conversations.

Check for Understanding Examples	
What I hear you say is . . .	Thanks for sharing from your heart about . . .
What I heard you share is . . .	Restate something and ask, "Is that correct?"

Checks for understanding slow down the conversation for true understanding to take place. Checks can be done as the listener or the sharer. After I learned this skill from Jorgensen, when I was working with my son and daughter, I would ask them, "What did you hear me say and what does it mean for you?" I realized that these two simple questions clarified what I was saying and it helped me make sure they were hearing what I wanted them to know and what it meant to them. Now, my own kids know this and will often smile when I ask it. These checks for understanding are essential when we are having learning conversations about walkthroughs, observations, meetings, or informal conversations. Whether you are the listener or the one sharing, make sure to use a check for understanding. Now, you don't need to use these in every conversation but once you begin to use them, they will feel more authentic and helpful. I must admit, it was a little awkward at first; but once I got used to it, I found this strategy so helpful. I will regularly use these checks for understanding when I am listening to students, staff, and parents. It's important to me that I understand what the person is saying and that I value their viewpoint by working to understand it.

Tell Me More

In addition to a check for understanding, one of my favorite conversation tools is to say, "Tell me more." During a conversation, as I listen for understanding I will ask the person to "tell me more" when they come to a pause. Let's take the teacher that was having the problem in their class from the story above, after the teacher shared that this student was frustrating them because they were acting out in class, I'd follow up the conversation by asking them to "tell me more." If needed, I'd ask clarifying questions like, "What specifically is the student doing that frustrates you?" When they share the behaviors, I'd ask them to tell me more. This one simple phrase, "tell me more," extends the conversation and allows the person to open up. It shows you are listening intently and are serious to learn more about the conversation. Below are some more "tell me more" phrases that you can use.

Tell Me More Examples	
I'd like to hear more about . . .	Please expound on . . .
Talk to me more about . . .	Share some more about . . .

When we focus and extend the conversation, deeper understanding is more likely to take place. This is extremely helpful when someone who comes to you is agitated, frustrated, or angry; it slows down the conversation as you check for understanding and ask them to tell you more. Frequently, listening, checking for understanding, and asking them to tell you more can de-escalate their emotions so they can begin to think and speak more clearly. Slowing down the conversation is important; take your time. Allow the person to vent; let them get it off their chest; and don't interject, interrupt, or try to convince them that their thinking is skewed. Instead, slow down the process, allow them to share, listen intently, check for understanding, and ask them to tell you more.

Speak From the Heart

If you work with middle school students you know they have a "Spidey" sense with their ability to tell if someone is genuine and speaking from the heart. They can see right through someone who is not being real with them. As we converse with others, it's important that we speak from the heart. Don't be afraid to speak from your heart, because this is how you truly build sustaining relationships anchored on trust. Let's take the teacher example again: When that teacher is sharing with you, be sure to be in the moment, check for understanding, ask them to tell you more, and speak from the heart. You could share a personal story with the teacher about a similar situation where a student had you at wit's end because of their behavior and how you were able to work through it.

We need to make our conversations more heartfelt, more genuine, and more nurturing. Even when I need to give someone bad news (e.g., discipline, suspension, dismissal), I do so in a caring, respectful, and heartfelt manner. All of us have to hold tough conversations with teachers about their performance, students about their negative behavior, or even parents over their actions, but I always strive to do so while speaking from my heart in a caring, loving, and respectful way. These conversations are tough, real tough, but I found that when you do this in a "speak from the heart" kind of way, people respect and hear you more. Trust me, this isn't easy; it takes practice and intention. It's so easy to get pulled into the cold, distant, and professional talk that says the same thing but is received so differently. Even if I need to expel a student, I work with the students and parents, and talk with them. I also follow up by giving all parties my cell phone number and encourage them to call me if I can ever help in any way.

Speaking from the heart is not something you will learn in a college class, and not many books speak about it, but I can tell you that this is one of the most transformational things that we can do as school leaders when in conversations with others. We need to realize the teacher you are talking to is someone's spouse, the student is someone's child, and the parent is someone's family. I find myself working to treat them like I would want the school leader treating my kids or wife. We need to surrender the tough-guy mentalities and embrace the need to care, love, respect, and nurture those we come in contact with hope and inspiration.

I especially like to think of hope when talking to someone who is struggling. Hope focuses on the future and doesn't limit someone to their past mistakes. I work to speak hope into students, parents, and staff members. By doing this, I'm working to inspire them to move forward through difficult times and to see that their future is bright and promising.

Suspend Certainty/Judgment

Jorgensen, my school leader coach, knows this is one of my hardest skills to work on. Too frequently, as someone is talking to me, I am jumping to conclusions, trying to solve their problem, or coming up with my own outcome. He would tell me to slow down the process and to suspend certainty. By doing this, I find now that I am more able to listen intently to the conversation without jumping to a conclusion. It also allows me to keep an open mind and allow for various conclusions, rather than the one that I quickly thought up.

Let's go back to the teacher who is frustrated because the student is acting out in their class. I have had this conversation many times, and before being coached by Jorgensen I would find myself either solving the problem in my mind, thinking of strategies I want to share with the teacher, thinking about how I could work with the student, or I would begin to make judgments about the teacher or student. Now, I work to suspend my own certainty and to suspend judgment. This allows me to listen as the teacher shares and it provides an opportunity for the two of us to work collaboratively toward a common goal.

Think about it: How many times have you been talking to someone when you find yourself thinking, "If they would only do this," "I could solve this problem," "I can't believe they didn't think of . . . ," "That's a great idea," or "This is a dumpster fire." I caution you to slow down the conversation and to suspend certainty and judgment. When we suspend certainty and judgment, it allows the conversation to further develop, the relationship between both parties to strengthen, and true collaboration around a common idea or goal to emerge.

Here's another aspect to consider: It's dangerous to want things for other people; it's vital to allow people to self-discover or collaborate together toward a common goal. Many times, school leaders are trying to be helpful and are constantly giving out recommendations and ways to improve when it's best to allow the person to self-discover. However, when the person self-discovers they are more likely to implement the action than if you told them how to do it. This heightens the need to suspend certainty and judgment when talking with others. It's very similar to the way we want students to own their learning instead of simply supplying answers for them.

From personal experience, I can tell you this isn't easy. I consciously remind myself during conversations to not come to my own conclusions, to suspend certainty and judgment. But, I can tell you, when you practice these on a consistent basis, your conversations and outcomes become so much stronger and richer.

Hold Space for Difference

During conversations, you will inevitably disagree or see a different perspective at some point. Holding space for difference is the skill of respecting someone's viewpoint even when you don't agree with it. It's also allowing for differences of opinion to come up in conversation and not working to convince someone of your viewpoint. School leaders need to know when to allow the space for difference. Take our teacher again. You are conversing with the teacher about the student and how they are demanding the student be taken out of their class because the student is frustrating them so much that they can't focus on their lessons. As a school leader, you believe it's important that the teacher learns to work through this challenge and that the student remains in the class. Allow space for differences and work to provide support for the teacher to thrive in the situation. Provide the teacher with strategies, connect them with a coach, or you coach them with classroom management strategies. Offer to schedule a meeting with the teacher, student, and student's parents to work toward a resolution.

Hold your ground because it's important that you stand for what you believe. But make sure you follow the above steps of the conversation that we shared earlier. Allow space to come back and discuss the topic again, reflect, take time to ponder, and marinate on the ideas. When we hold space for differences, we are willing to not convince the person to our viewpoint but we are able to reflect, take a step back, and support them where they are.

This can also be a challenging skill in conversations because school leaders like to find resolution or consensus around a topic or discussion. It can be difficult to hold space for differences, but it's mission critical. Plus, it builds trust, respect, and relationships that are sustaining. Figure 1.1 shows a matrix that can help focus your work with the skills we discussed and turn conversation into your most powerful leadership tool.

As you complete the simulation at the end of the chapter, use Figure 1.1 to see how you are doing in developing meaningful conversations with your staff.

Figure 1.1 Meaningful Conversations

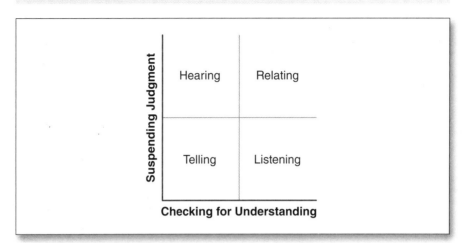

MORE MEANINGFUL MEETINGS

School leaders are constantly leading meetings, conferences, faculty meetings, and conversations with groups of people. To be a successful leader you need to run meetings in a manner that is collaborative and focuses on an outcome that is clear, attainable, and focused.

Before starting any meeting, it's meaningful to start with a Check-In. A Check-In allows each person's voice be heard in the group, and it engages each member of the meeting in a quick, personable, and conversational way. The Check-In is a simple question that each member is asked collectively as a group and then asked to share out with the group, depending on its size, or with a partner(s).

The Check-In works best when it's related to the topic of the meeting, but it doesn't always have to connect. Sometimes the most powerful Check-In opportunities are more group building in nature and allow people to refocus their attention from the dozens of thoughts running through their mind as they assemble for the meeting.

To provide focus and clarity in the meeting, I like to use the Context, Purpose, and Outcome strategy (see Figure 1.2). This is another skill my coach has worked with me on to strengthen my ability to run meetings. I found that by using this skill, meetings are more efficient and focused.

It's important to set the Context before the meeting. The Context sets circumstances around the topic or situation that is being discussed. Let's imagine that you are running a faculty meeting about state testing procedures that have been revamped by the state. The state is now mandating that all schools administer their exams online. The Context might be, "As you may have heard, the state is now requiring us to administer the state

Samples of Check-Ins	
Tell us what you think the most important aspect of classroom management is . . .	The one thing I'm thinking about the most after reading this article for today is . . .
High-stakes testing has resulted in . . .	I am most inspired by . . .
The event (home or work) I'm looking forward to in the next few months is . . .	Where does this article "square up" with your own experiences as a leader?

math and ELA exams online. In light of that mandate we will have to seriously consider the gaps in our technology infrastructure." The Context describes the background or current situation and it provides the setting or framework for why the topic is being discussed.

The next piece to highlight is the Purpose of the meeting. This explains the reason behind the meeting. Using the state testing mandate, the Purpose may be, "The purpose of today's meeting is to discuss and review the state's mandate on math and ELA testing and come up with a plan to address our wireless network." The Purpose provides a laser focus on the intent of the meeting and it serves as a guide throughout the meeting to keep the participants on topic. If the meeting begins to get off point, the school leader can guide the meeting back to the purpose simply by saying, "Let's get back to our Purpose for today's meeting." It's always good to write down the Purpose for others to see.

The final piece is to identify the Outcome of the meeting. This is the result, product, or final decision from the Context and Purpose. Staying with our state testing example, the Outcome could be, "The team will design a testing protocol and testing schedule for administering the online practice test before the state assessment window begins." The school leader needs to come back to the Outcome and work to reflect on it with all participants. The strongest outcomes are ones that are collaborative, team centered, and personalized for each member. Each member of the meeting needs to play a role in the Outcome for it to be owned and implemented.

Creative Tension

The difference in where your organization currently exists and the condition you would like it to attain creates a useful dissonance that researchers identify as creative tension (Senge, 2006). Another way to illustrate this is with the simple question, "Where are we, and where do we want to be?" One research study speaks of creative tension and notes, "The researcher is not suggesting the creation of an atmosphere, climate, or culture that places unhealthy expectations or environments upon administrators,

Figure 1.2 CPO Ladder

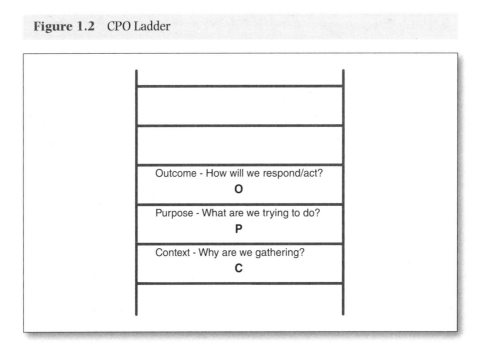

Outcome - How will we respond/act?

O

Purpose - What are we trying to do?

P

Context - Why are we gathering?

C

teachers, or students. The desired tension is a positive, cognitive, visionary tension that exists when one is keenly aware of their own practice, an authentic, systemic need, and how their improved practice could become a vital part of the creative, continuous improvement to address that need" (Ramage, 2007). This sense of aspiring to be better, to be something else, can lead to fertile innovation and creativity. We'll talk more about the use of questioning to assist this process in Chapter 6.

SCHOOL CULTURE

School culture rises and falls on the relationships that are built in it. If school leaders want to engage all learners, inspire teachers, and encourage parents they need to be highly relational. My good friend and colleague Matt Saferite, former Breaking Ranks principal of Bentonville High School and now director of assessment, says, "Culture is everything, it's the core of your school and where true learning is nurtured and takes place. Without a positive and caring culture, your school can't move forward."

When a school culture is relational, caring, nurturing, and respectful, all students and adults in the school community are free to live out the core mission, vision, and core values of the school. A relational culture is a safe place to engage all learners (students and adults) and work to connect each person to the larger community.

Never underestimate the power of frequent, focused, and meaningful conversations to grow the kind of culture you want for your school. Culture doesn't happen by accident because relationships don't happen by accident. It's why we start the book with this chapter, and why it underpins all other aspects of the work we will discuss. We encourage you to treat our ideas as ongoing conversation. We will listen for understanding as you participant in online opportunities that will expand our conversation. Our intention is to have that ongoing conversation, not for you to endure a 10-chapter lecture and walk away. It's an exciting time to be a school leader, and if we are going to be successful we all need to keep talking to one another.

We encourage every reader to participate in ongoing conversation at www.chaselearning.org. This site allows us to slow down the conversation, check for understanding, and build the kind of professional relationships needed for our collective success—success that ensures our students, families, and communities gain the kinds of learning opportunities needed to thrive in their future world.

Take time at the end of this chapter to participate in an online simulation that will challenge your leadership skills and provide some thought-provoking dialogue and reflection for you and your fellow school leaders.

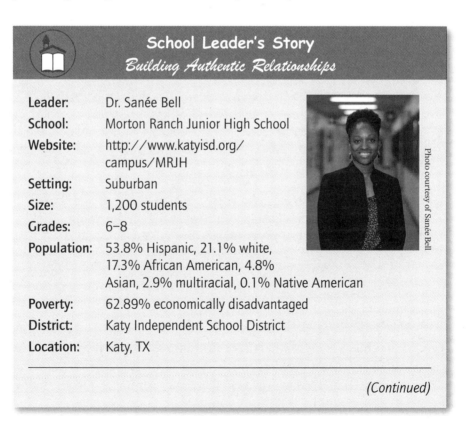

School Leader's Story
Building Authentic Relationships

Leader:	Dr. Sanée Bell
School:	Morton Ranch Junior High School
Website:	http://www.katyisd.org/campus/MRJH
Setting:	Suburban
Size:	1,200 students
Grades:	6–8
Population:	53.8% Hispanic, 21.1% white, 17.3% African American, 4.8% Asian, 2.9% multiracial, 0.1% Native American
Poverty:	62.89% economically disadvantaged
District:	Katy Independent School District
Location:	Katy, TX

Photo courtesy of Sanée Bell

(Continued)

(Continued)

Dr. Bell shares that visibility is key for every school leader. "Visibility is really important—high visibility and an open-door policy." She understands this sounds simple and cliché but admits that so many school leaders devalue the power of visibility in building relationships. Dr. Bell is passionate about building relationships and hearing from students. She shares the value she places on relationships saying, "Nothing significant can take place without a trusting and collaborative relationship." To build relationships she hosts a student roundtable to hear from students on ways she can support them and get feedback on the school. The students on this roundtable serve as her advisory group to hear how they can work to improve the school. She also hosts new-student lunches to welcome them to the school. During these lunches she asks the following questions:

- How are things going at our school?
- What do you wish we did differently?
- Do you have any ideas or suggestions to improve our school?

Dr. Bell follows up the student lunches by calling their parents to welcome them to the school and to solicit their feedback.

Most recently, Dr. Bell started "Student Feedback Cards" to ask students what are the two things they are most proud of with their school. On the back of the card they share ways that the school can improve. She and the staff review every card and work to celebrate the areas of pride—and strategize to strengthen the areas needing improvement.

Dr. Bell also serves as a mentor to one of the students on her school campus. "This provides me the opportunity to invest in the student's life and to coach them to success and growth." Connecting with a student to mentor, encourage, and advise them is a powerful way to build relationships that make a real, lasting difference.

"My success is rooted and grounded in my ability to build authentic relationships with teachers, students, and parents that inspire them to become something greater collectively that would not otherwise be possible alone."

—Dr. Sanée Bell

Key Chapter Takeaways

Every school has dreams of what they can be, aspirations for their future. The relationships between the leaders and everyone involved will be a key element in how successful any school will be in reaching their hopes and dreams for the future. This chapter shows the power of conversation for the critical work of leading. The work of Peter Senge, Ray Jorgensen, and Margaret Wheatley reminds us to keep the conversation going. The simple acting of turning and talking with each other is at the heart of building, and growing, relationships. These relationships are central to nurturing the culture we want to create (Jorgensen & Hurst, 2009; Senge, 2006; Wheatley, 1994).

Make time to have focused conversations with the skills and tools highlighted in Chapter 1. We use these strategies and we've seen them make a substantial difference in our own teams and schools. One of the great by-products of this process is how each person involved will feel when they've truly been heard. This simple act of listening to each other is at the heart of conversational leadership.

RELATE, INNOVATE, INVIGORATE ACTIVITIES

Relate

- Design a Content, Purpose, Outcome (CPO) strategy for the next meeting you will be facilitating.
- Design a Check-In for your next meeting.
- Practice listening for understanding in your next faculty meeting using this exercise:

Break the group into pairs. Give this prompt to the group: "What got you into education? And what keeps you here?" Each person will have two minutes to answer the prompt, and two minutes to listen to their partner. While listening you may only say two things: "Tell me more" and "I don't understand." Debrief with the group and focus on the experience of listening and being heard.

Innovate

- Consider a Check-In that has a direct connection to the content of the meeting instead of a more "relational" or ice-breaker style.
- Focus on doing a check for understanding at least three times today.
- Use Figure 1.1 to reflect on a recent conversation. Do a self-assessment of where you think that conversation lands on the grid.

Invigorate

- Speak From the Heart – Share your passion, speak the truth, and let your staff see your heart.

- Speak Words of Encouragement – Be intentional today about encouraging three students and staff members.
- Suspend Judgment – Pause before judging or drawing conclusions.

Team Talk: Relate

Meet with your core leadership team and share stories of people who inspired your leadership style and made a difference in your leadership. Go to **www.chaselearning.org/TeamTalk** to share your story (in 100 words or less) of what you learned or experienced through this Team Talk activity.

SCHOOL LEADER SIMULATION (SIM): THE BULLY TEACHER

Go to **www.chaselearning.org** to access the SIM.

This School Leader Simulation (SIM) is a web-based activity that will challenge school leaders to work together as a team to solve a realistic scenario played out on the web. This SIM will challenge your communication and decision-making process. It is best completed by a team, discussing various options, decision making, and thought processes. It is our hope that you will find this SIM engaging and thought provoking.

Continue the conversation with us on Twitter at #chaselearning.

Communication Builds Community

Telling Your School Story Together

> *"Be sure to proofread—especially when communicating from portable devices. If you blindly trust autocorrect or push two virtual keys in the wrong order the importance of your message can be ruined."*
>
> —Bill and Dave

*I*n this chapter we focus on the tenet that communication builds community. You will learn about branding your school and gain tools and strategies to use right away to build community through increased communication. Communication allows community members to be connected to your school and helps them support your school's mission and students. Most of all, communication extends the reach of your school beyond the school walls and unites students, teachers, and staff members around a common purpose and focus. The digital tools we'll feature are easily accessible—often free—and won't require a graduate course to understand or use them.

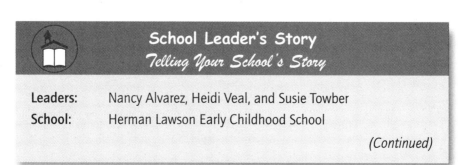

School Leader's Story
Telling Your School's Story

Leaders:	Nancy Alvarez, Heidi Veal, and Susie Towber
School:	Herman Lawson Early Childhood School

(Continued)

(Continued)

Website: http://www.schools.mckinneyisd.net/lawson/

Setting: Suburban

Size: 700 students

Grades: PreK (Ages 3–5)

Population: 59.1% Hispanic, 18.3% white, 14.8% African American, 3.6% Asian, 3.0% multiracial, 1.0% Native American, 0.2% Pacific Islander

Poverty: 75.2% economically disadvantaged

District: McKinney Independent School District

Location: McKinney, TX

Photo courtesy of Nancy Alvarez

Photo courtesy of Heidi Veal

The leaders and teachers at Lawson Early Childhood School, a bilingual campus, leverage social media to build trust with parents, staff, and the community. School leader Nancy Alvarez shares, "Social media makes the walls of your school transparent. That transparency builds trust with the families and the community we serve. It shows there is nothing to hide; on the contrary, we are able to highlight everything we are doing and focus on the positive." For example, teachers at Lawson use social media to share exactly what is going on in classrooms. They video classroom lessons and then post them on private Facebook pages for parents, who are then able to replicate lessons at home, question students to extend or review concepts, and have meaningful conversations about what takes place at school. Teachers also share individual successes and milestones on goals through apps like Seesaw and Bloomz so parents can celebrate these accomplishments at home. Feedback from families about this popular, easy-to-access communication is immensely positive.

Social media has also allowed Lawson to increase participation in school-wide community functions. Before social media, events might be attended by as few as 30 people, whereas those promoted through a schoolwide Facebook page and Remind now might see 600 in attendance. Administrators and teachers make commercials that are posted on Facebook for families so parents have a better understanding of what will be shared at these events. Parents see the enthusiasm from the staff and feel they are receiving a personal invitation to attend. Additionally, the staff makes YouTube announcements to motivate students to attend, and parents are reminded of the event on classroom social media pages, call-outs, and Remind. After each function, pictures are posted on Facebook. The comments are very positive, encouraging even more parents to attend subsequent events.

Last year on the school's Facebook page, Heidi Veal, a Lawson assistant principal, posted a picture of one of Lawson's bus drivers with the caption, "We love our bus drivers." Suddenly and quite organically, parents started commenting about their favorite drivers and positive moments shared with them. Now, new Lawson parents who may be apprehensive about allowing their preschooler to ride a bus are directed to the Lawson Facebook page where they read what Lawson families say about the bus drivers and how wonderful they are. Facebook analytics reveal that this particular Facebook post has been viewed over 700 times. Social media has clearly helped Lawson build the community's trust through transparency.

Communication preferences are determined at Lawson home visits. Every child/family receives at least one home visit a year to deepen the relationship and build trust with the parents and the student. At the student's home, teachers share information about the school, classroom, and curriculum. Parents also complete an important survey about how they would like to receive communication from the school and their teacher. Overwhelmingly, survey results reveal that parents prefer to receive information on Facebook. Teachers also take a moment to ask parents two important questions: "What are your hopes for your child at Lawson this year?" and "What are your fears for your child at Lawson?" Surprisingly, most answers are similar; the majority of parents want to know that their children are safe, loved, and having fun learning. As a result, Lawson filters every social media post through the lens of those three important factors.

In addition to Facebook, Lawson uses Remind to communicate with parents, who can sign up to receive updates, newsletters, and other information from the school in English, Spanish, or both. In fact, all communication with parents, oral and written, is provided in English and in Spanish. In this way, Lawson values all its families.

> "A través de la comunicación, desarrollemos una relación de confianza y colaboración con nuestras familias [We use communication to build trust and to encourage collaboration with our families]."
>
> —Nancy Alvarez

BRANDING YOUR SCHOOL

If you are not telling your school's story, someone else will! Have you ever heard a colleague or staff member say something like, "There's such good learning going on at our school, but all we ever hear about in the press are the shortcomings of our high-stakes testing results or behavior issues with a few of our most challenging students"? These comments could easily be the comments of many school leaders across the country.

As a school leader, it is imperative to engage your community through regular, professional, and relevant communication produced in a variety of formats. Branding your school refers to communicating with a consistent and creative theme, your school's mission and core values, celebrations, and school life. When school leaders work to brand their school, they need to collaborate with all members of the school community to assure that a well-rounded plan is developed.

Regular Communication

With the ease of communication via social media, community members expect up-to-the-minute reports on school activities. Whether it be scores at an athletic event, live streaming from musical concerts, tweeting out various classroom activities, or posting cool things happening in the school on social media, participants have an insatiable appetite for an inside look at your school. When school leaders provide regular and timely updates on the school, the community begins to be engaged and involved in the life of the school. Below are some examples on how school leaders can provide regular communication.

Newsletters

A carefully crafted school newsletter should be communicating your school's mission, purpose, celebrations, needs, important dates, and information, and serve as an eye into school life on a regular basis. *Regular* refers to this letter going out on an expected timeline, whether it be weekly, biweekly, or monthly. Whatever frequency you choose, the important thing is to stick with it; newsletters that are sporadic are often not read and frequently discarded in inboxes. However, a regular newsletter builds a relationship with the reader that connects them with the school and the writer. More often than not, school newsletters are all print and are not designed with the reader in mind. We are big believers that less is more in this case—less print and more pictures and videos. This is where school leaders need to have the eye of a marketer, writer, reporter, and publisher when designing newsletters. Consider catchy titles that attract the eye, pictures that showcase your mission or topic, and keep the writing relational in context. Later in this chapter, we will share a powerful tool that will make any school leader appear to be a skilled graphic designer when creating their school newsletter. Smore.com provides what they term as beautiful and easy-to-design newsletters. Creating an online newsletter allows school leaders to get multiple use, and extended readership, from a single communication tool. An online newsletter allows school leaders to post it on their website, Twitter page, Facebook wall, and attach in e-mails. Newsletters are easy to archive and they showcase your school's successes over a school year. Extend the use of your newsletter beyond students, parents, and educators. Use the newsletter to showcase your school to realtors, businesses, senior citizens, churches, and as many taxpayers as you can. This builds a community's belief in their school system, increases communication with the school, and builds partnerships that will support students in their learning. Since school choice has increased the competitive nature of public schooling, it's important to be sharing your school newsletter with parents of students that live in your school's jurisdiction but do not attend your school. For example, consider creating an e-mailing list of students who attend cyber-school and don't attend your school; use your newsletter to highlight the exciting things going on at your school to these prospective parents.

School Goals/Progress

School leaders can benefit greatly when they provide parents and community members regular updates on their school's goals and progress. This can include a quarterly or biannual review of the school's goals and their progress in regard to student achievement. Develop a transparent communication for parents, students, and educators that highlights the school's successes, challenges, areas needing improvement, and future dreams and goals. By doing this, it allows the community members to participate and contribute to the school's mission. For instance, if one of your school's goals is to create a Makerspace, clearly list your material needs and resources desired to complete this goal. You just may have a community that will invest in your project, supply materials, or offer to volunteer career expertise in helping you reach your goal. Don't forget to showcase student work in these reports. End of unit projects, number of books read, art gallery, science fair, or math progress data are just some of the things that can be included. Brand the report by calling it a catchy name that connects with your school and the mission of the report. Continue to use this same name every time you publish a school progress update. Consistent naming helps guide the reader in knowing what to expect, and supports your school's branding. A standard report format will help readers know what to expect each time the report is published.

School Leader Blog

When school leaders blog, it engages the community with them and it allows for a targeted focus toward one topic. Blogging allows the school leader to laser focus the message that they desire community members to be reading. A blog also provides a way for readers to interact and share their ideas in a two-way conversation. Here are a few blogs that take advantage of a digital format for learning with parents and community members:

Matt Renwick

https://readingbyexample.com/

Mineral Point Elementary School
Mineral Point, WI

Photo courtesy of Matt Renwick

Matt Renwick is an elementary principal in Wisconsin. He is a leader in innovation and leadership for school leaders. In his two blogs, he provides practical and real-life strategies on digital literacy. Check out Renwick's other blog on Literacy, Leadership, and Technology.

Bobby Dodd

http://glhsprincipal.blogspot.com/

Gahannah Lincoln High School
Gahannah, OH

This practical blog showcases the work of the high school; provides tips for parents, students, and teachers; and challenges the status quo in regard to digital leadership. Dodd is a motivator and this shines through in his blog posts. A 2016 NASSP (National Association of Secondary School Principals) Digital Principal Award winner, he is a leader on digital leadership nationwide.

Todd Nesloney

http://www.toddnesloney.com/class-blog

Brule Elementary School
Navasota, TX

Without a doubt, Todd Nesloney is one of the most energizing school leaders that is committed to inspiring educators to care about kids. He is the cofounder of Kids Deserve It! His blog provides strategies for flipped classrooms, digital tools, and simple ways to have fun as a school leader. I also encourage you to check out Kids Deserve It at http://www.kidsdeserveit.com/ to learn to have fun as a school leader.

Social Media

Did you know that if the number of account holders of Facebook was a country it would be the third-largest country in the world—behind only China and India. Twitter would be the fourth-largest country, and Instagram is catching up in popularity. More people every day are joining these social networks, and school leaders need to harness this popularity by posting regular and timely updates on social media. Give community members a glimpse into your school day by posting pics of students, teachers, staff members, and student work. Set a goal of publishing at least one social media post each day. Or, commit to posting at least once a week. Regularity is important as it builds momentum and expectations for the community member. A stagnant social media presence can actually break down a school's engagement with its community. Post event dates and times, key information, and news for your school. But more importantly, use social media to engage the reader with your school's daily life, mission, and purpose. This medium is perfect to build relationships with community members and highlight the relationships that are being established in your school. In all honesty, most people who are on social media are looking for more of a relational approach to your school's postings. Stories about the achievements of students, pictures of teachers and staff members connecting with students, and video clips of students showcasing their learning are all things that will harvest a large following and engage the community.

Use social media to take the participant behind the scenes of your school. Below are some examples to help school leaders go behind the scenes to engage their community:

- Post live video of a school assembly or activity
- Stream live from a classroom presentation or lesson
- Share behind-the-scenes pictures and interviews before the school concert, play, or sporting event

There's nothing like a hotly contested sporting event, an elementary school concert, or an after-school event like a dance, prom, reading roundup, grandparents' day, or father–daughter dance to increase community engagement with your social media presence. Use these events to build anticipation by posting reminders that you will be posting score updates, live video from the concert, and pics from that special evening event. Encourage parents to engage with the postings by sharing them with their friends, commenting, and liking the post. Take advantage of the big events in your school by building up anticipation for these events and encouraging members to follow along. Think of it this way: Your live video feed of the elementary school concert may allow the mom who is on a business trip out of the country to see her son singing his heart out or the dad that's in the hospital fighting an illness to see his daughter score the winning goal, and it will allow the grandparent to watch their grandchild walk across the stage at the promotion ceremony.

We will talk further on the use of social media in schools, but for this section, we want you to remember these key points: Social media needs to be regular, frequent, relational, and focused. When school leaders use social media in this manner, the community gets engaged, your school is strengthened, and parents are more confident in you as a leader. The school is telling their own story.

Urgent Updates

Without a doubt, one of the most important ways to build confidence in a school leader is to provide regular, timely, and up-to-the-minute updates during a time of crisis, urgency, or emergency within the school. "Leadership within schools plays a pivotal role to ensuring the safety and well-being of all students and staff" (Ziegler, 2005). There is nothing like a parent hearing from their kids before they hear from you about something that is going at the school. Whether it be the need to evacuate the school, a lockdown, a medical emergency, or crisis in your school building, parents and community members expect regular and timely updates. These updates can be difficult for school leaders to publish as they simultaneously deal with a crisis on site, but we wanted to provide you with some tools and ideas to strengthen your communication during a crisis.

Delegate Select someone, preferably someone not in your school but at central office or another school, to receive timely updates via cell phone or walkie talkie and post updates to your school's social media accounts. This designee will send out e-mails and phone calls to parents, and serve as a calm, articulate, and informed reporter for you and your school. This is another example of telling your story before someone else tells the wrong story!

Templates We understand that you can never predict what is going to happen or know the type of crisis that will take place in your school. What we can predict is that at one point, every school will have some type of emergency. We encourage school leaders to have templates, or sample messages, that can be tweaked or adjusted to communicate the event that is taking place at the school. We suggest creating sample templates for the following emergencies: Medical Emergency, Evacuation, Weather Alert

Emergency, and Emergency in the Community But Near the School. By designing these templates in a calm time in collaboration with your district administration and local law enforcement, school leaders will engage the community in a way that will help to calm their fears, slow down the rumor mill, and provide confidence in you as a school leader.

Professional

In today's media-saturated culture, design matters! Quality content will often go unread unless the design engages the reader. School community members expect a professional approach to communications. With a school leader's busy schedule, taking the time to design, create, and produce high-quality professional communications is challenging. However, below are some key digital tools that can help any school leader look like a professional designer.

DIGITAL MEDIA TOOLS

Smore.com (free and paid version): Smore provides school leaders an easy-to-use, intuitive, and totally web-based environment for newsletters and flyers. This is one of our favorite tools to create professional, innovative, and relational newsletters and flyers for schools. The free version allows users to create a handful of newsletters at no cost. They also have a paid version just for educators that allows unlimited newsletters and a plethora of resources. Smore is free of advertisements, and archives all newsletters for quick and easy access. Once you join as an educator, you can participate in Hive, the educational community on Smore.com. In the Hive, you can see what other educators are doing to brand their school.

- Easy Design and Editing: Smore makes it easy for the digital novice and the tech guru school leader. Smore's editing is intuitive and customizable. It gives you the ability to customize your own background, and add pictures, videos, and links. There are several backgrounds that are part of the education subscription and a variety of themed backgrounds, which change seasonally.
- Assorted Media: It's easy to embed video, upload pics, and share links that automatically turn into a button that readers can click on. The button feature is nice because it allows the writer to create a button readers can click on and link to a website.
- Analytics: By far, this is one of our favorite components of Smore. School leaders will be able to collect live data such as who opens the newsletter, geotracking of readers, what buttons the reader clicks

on, e-mail bounce-backs, number of times the newsletter has been opened, and much more.

- E-mail Distribution List: School leaders can create e-mail distribution lists within Smore. The paid version allows school leaders to send 5,000 e-mails a month. When using the e-mail distribution list, school leaders can track the e-mail accounts that opened the newsletter. Smore publications can also be e-mailed as a link using your district's communication resources.
- Invitations: These newsletters also provide a sign-up or registration for special events, which comes with directions to the event.

Typically, school leaders are not trained as graphic designers, but the ability to communicate in a manner that engages the reader through creative, innovative, and relational publications is an essential future focused skill for all school leaders. The next digital tool provides an easy, intuitive, and excellent resource for school leaders to design professional-looking documents, designs, and images.

Canva (www.canva.com; free and paid versions): This is a simply awesome graphic design tool that is easy to use and will make any school leader look professional in their branding. Canva is a graphic design platform that helps school leaders design beautiful images and documents.

- Documents: Create banners, social media, and more.
- Customizable: Design your word art, info graphics, flyers, logos, etc.
- Education Community: Canva has an active educational community that includes lesson plans, ideas for visual literacy, and much more.
- Workshops: Canva provides workshops in graphic designing for educators. This professional development can help school leaders identify ways to creatively engage their readers with images using this powerful graphic design tool.
- Extensive Resources: Canva literally has over a million images that you can use to communicate your message. In addition to these images, it allows you to filter, edit, and customize free icons and shapes with over 100 different fonts that will sharpen any written graphic.
- Backgrounds: There are thousands of background images and wallpapers that designers can select from. The rich collection of educational images supports branding for school leaders.

Adobe Spark (https://spark.adobe.com): This digital tool is transforming how people design media and videos. Its slogan is "Create impactful social graphics, web stories, and animated videos using Spark's free graphic design app." This app and website allows school leaders to design high-quality media that can be used in their school.

- Easy to Use: This app is so easy to use any digital newcomer could master it in a short time.
- Spark Post: Spark Post allows the creation of social graphics that will take any picture and add words, graphics, and filters to strengthen the message.
- Spark Page: This tool equips school leaders with the ability to design web stories. Turn words and images into beautiful, magazine-style web stories that will impress readers on any device.
- Animated Videos: Bring your videos to life by personalizing the content, delivery, and messaging. There is a library of photos, icons, and soundtracks to add to your video to create that professional image.
- Templates: Adobe Spark provides users with templates that can be easily accessed and personalized with your own message. A good selection of backgrounds and fonts is available to use, and there is a sizable library of photos, filters, and soundtracks to choose from.
- Editing: Even though you can personalize or use their templates, the user has the ability to edit and change the image and text to meet their needs. Whether it's blurring the background, changing the font, adding a title to your message, or filtering the final product, Adobe Spark provides these tools and many more.
- Sharing: Once finished with the text graphic, Adobe Spark allows you to send the final product to social media (Instagram, Twitter, Facebook, Tumblr, Pinterest, e-mail, and text).

In addition to Adobe Spark, here are some easy-to-use digital tools that allow school leaders to communicate in a creative, innovative, and relational manner. These tools will make infographics, chart design, and text graphics easy for any level of digital user.

MentiMeter (https://www.mentimeter.com/): This is one of our favorite tools to engage participants while you are presenting. It allows the user to have their audience create word clouds, multiple-choice, quizzes, scales, open-ended questions, and competitions through matrix games. This tool is easy to use, intuitive for the participant, and provides great analytics.

Easelly (http://www.easel.ly): Easelly equips school leaders with an infographic tool that can turn data, important information, or statistics into an infographic for readers. Easelly has free and paid versions. The free version provides you with the ability to create infographics, and the monthly paid version is a nominal fee but it opens a huge library of graphics, sample templates, fonts, and thousands of free images.

RELEVANCE

The final piece to engage community members through communication is to ensure that school leaders are communicating a relevant message that resonates with the community and reflects the school mission, goals, and life. Great school leaders know relevant communication shares what the reader needs to know and what that reader wants to know. Relevant communication is also distributed in a customizable manner so the receiver selects the best options for them to engage with the content. In this section, school leaders will learn about the most powerful digital communication tools to revolutionize the way we communicate and engage the school community. The ability to engage community members through communication is a future focused skill that will increase in need and demand as we continue to lead.

Need to Know

School leaders need to communicate key information to community members in a redundant, creative, and innovative manner. Too often, information gets drowned out in communication through tons of print or too much fluff that does not meet the needs of the recipient. Here are some tips to make key information pop out to community members and to stick in their minds once they are finished.

- Redundant: Saying the same message in a variety of mediums, frequencies, and formats is critical. If possible, include your key information in a newsletter, blog, text, and phone call home. For example, if your elementary school is on a two-hour delay because of teacher professional development, keep the message running in your weekly newsletter for weeks, and send a text and phone call about a month before the day and then again within a few days of the delay. This helps to prepare the community about the delay and it helps them in planning.
- Succinct: Try to shorten your announcement and provide an area where community members can go to to learn more about the announcement.

Want to Know

This is where you showcase your school and the exciting things that are taking place with your students, staff, and faculty members. Use students and faculty/staff to help school leaders engage the community and your school. Below are some tools and strategies that school leaders can use to engage the community in what they want to know. School leaders need to break down the school walls and open the schoolhouse doors to engage the community in entirely new ways. This requires creativity, a focused approach, and a commitment to encouraging innovation by all members of the school community. This can be accomplished by the novice or veteran school leader with these easy-to-use and winsome digital tools.

- Seesaw (http://web.seesaw.me; free): Help parents get an inside look at their child's work with student online portfolios. Seesaw allows parents to view and interact with their own child's school work live during the school day. Seesaw has changed dinner-table conversations to focus on a discussion around the learning. School leaders can publish student work for parents and the community to view. This creates an authentic audience for the student, which is larger than the classroom and teacher.

- ClassDojo (https://www.classdojo.com; free): Engage students and keep parents in the loop. Parents can receive instant messages, pictures, announcements, and regular updates on their child's performance and behavior. This digital tool helps school leaders build community with parents, students, and teachers. It engages parents in the learning and behavior management of their child. ClassDojo also engages the learner by teaching teamwork, collaboration, and persistence.

- Twitter (www.twitter.com): Twitter is an excellent way to let community members see inside your school on a daily basis. In addition to regular, daily posts we mentioned earlier, try something new to give school community members an opportunity to learn more about your school.

- Twitter Takeover Day: Consider having a student and/or a teacher use the school's Twitter account to post about their day in school. To help this be successful, it's important to select a student who can be trusted and already has a strong following of fellow students. Twitter Teacher Takeover gives school community members a behind-the-scenes look at the life of a teacher, and it also builds the relationship between the school, teacher, and community. Here are some things to consider with Student and Teacher Twitter Takeover Days:

- ○ Clear Guidelines: It's important that guidelines on what to post, what not to post, and how to post are articulated. In regard to the student, a parent–student conference is a valuable tool to review expectations and to sign a contract stating that the student will comply with given guidelines.
- ○ Graphics: Since we know that a picture paints a thousand words, encourage the student and teacher to use pictures and video to showcase their day.
- ○ Learning: It can be so easy to get distracted with the Twitter Takeover Day that the learning is lost. Make sure that the teacher and student emphasize what is being learned by sharing problems, questions, and activities that are being completed in the classroom.
- ○ Relationships: Encourage the teacher and student to focus on the relationships that take place during the school day.
- ○ Media: Get help in promoting your Twitter Takeover Days. Send out a press release and be sure to Storify the Twitter Takeover Day for everyone to read and view.

- Instagram: Instagram is no longer just an app for teens to share their favorite pics. It is now a valuable tool for school leaders to engage the school community in an entirely new way. Below are some examples of how schools can use Instagram to promote learning and the school.

  - ○ Virtual Art Show: Create an Instagram account for your art department and showcase your artwork to the world. We were especially impressed how one school placed QR codes on student artwork and the QR code took viewers to a short video message from the student talking about their work. Another school used a time-lapsed video to show the artwork from start to finish.
  - ○ Showcase Student Work: Post a weekly Student Work feature on your school's Instagram account.
  - ○ School Branding: Instagram is an excellent tool to brand your school with inspiring messages, quotes from students and teachers, and reminders of important school events.

- Learning Management Systems (LMS): These classroom digital platforms provide school leaders with a collaborative tool with students, teachers, and parents. Plus, it increases communication by helping parents stay on top of their child's class assignments—arguably the one thing all parents want to know. A well-designed LMS helps students collaborate with fellow classmates around classroom lessons, and provides teachers with a platform to create blended learning opportunities. The LMS extends learning beyond the classroom walls and bell schedule. Many of these platforms serve as the learning environment for online classes, hybrid courses, and digital tools for collaboration. Blackboard, Moodle, Schoology, and Edmodo are four of these systems that are excellent and very popular for K–12 school systems throughout the country. Schoology and Edmodo are the more intuitive and accessible options from the four listed. If you do not currently have a learning management system available for your school, we suggest starting with a hosted service like Schoology. Learning management systems foster collaboration, promote student accountability, expand pedagogy, and increase parental oversight of their child's learning. Digital ecosystems, like the ones mentioned, are best used in a schoolwide platform. This is really no longer the future of education but the current status, as many of our nation's schools already use a digital learning management system. For school leaders to be future focused, they need to embrace these digital tools and use them to engage all students, parents, and educators.

- U.S. Department of Education Go Open (https://tech.ed.gov/open/): Its website states, "The #GoOpen campaign encourages states, school districts and educators to use openly licensed educational materials to transform teaching and learning. District and state leaders are working alongside innovators from education technology companies and nonprofit organizations to share effective strategies and ideas, create new tools and provide professional learning opportunities that help educators find, adapt, create, and share resources."

- Amazon Inspire (https://www.amazoninspire.com): At the International Society for Technology in Education's 2016 conference and expo, Amazon joined the #GoOpen effort and announced Amazon Inspire, a free service for the search, discovery, and distribution of digital educational resources. According to its press release, "Amazon Inspire, with its rich features such as search, discovery and peer reviews, will provide educators—regardless of funding or location—access to upload and share free digital teaching resources."

"Amazon joins educators from around the country in recognizing the power of digital learning to transform the classroom, by creating a personalized, engaging learning environment for all students," said Rohit Agarwal, general manager of Amazon K–12 Education. Amazon Inspire has five key tools: (1) Smart Search—Allows teachers to explore resources by grade level, standard, or content area;

(2) Collections—This feature allows educators to group resources into collections; (3) Simple Upload—Amazon Inspire allows educators to easily upload their work and resources; (4) Customer Reviews—Educators can rate and review resources on Amazon Inspire; and (5) Accessibility Support—Amazon Inspire has built-in accessibility features that allow educators to easily navigate to the resources and to indicate the accessibility features of resources they upload.

Best Communication Tool: Remind

Without a doubt, the best tool to communicate in a way that engages the entire school community is Remind. Remind (https://www.remind.com)  allows school leaders to reach students, parents, and educators where they are. Remind has revolutionized the way school leaders can communicate with the school community. It is free for school leaders and teachers, easy to use, and allows the user to get the information in the format they prefer. This digital tool empowers school leaders with the opportunity to communicate their message in a variety of ways, to different groups, and in multiple languages. Plus, we know that so many school leaders and school community members have full e-mail inboxes with e-mails that never get read. Remind sends a text or SMS message directly to the recipient's phone, causing a larger, more timely viewing experience.

We believe Remind is the best app to engage your school community because it's easy to use, includes text messaging/push technology to increase the chance of the recipient viewing the message, and provides a variety of resources to communicate your message. Plus, the targeted professional development and supportive Remind team both provide outstanding support features as you create your account, set up your Remind groups, and begin to send out your first set of messages. Most importantly, Remind builds and nurtures the relationship between the school leader and the school community. When this relationship is developed, the entire school community wins!

- Administrator Features: Allow school leaders to view all of the Remind groups in their school, send messages to teachers, review announcement histories, and view data on the number of communications sent.
- Easy to Use: Without a doubt, this is the easiest to use digital tool that we have ever worked with. Whether on a mobile device or a desktop, Remind.com is user friendly, intuitive, and natural to use.

Plus, Remind provides a rich tutoring tool to guide first-time users through the digital tool and how to set up and use Remind.

- Recipient Personalization: The person receiving the Remind message can determine if they want to receive the notice via text, e-mail, or push technology by using the mobile app. The school leader does not need to manage who gets in; all they need to do is send the Remind code and allow members to join or remove themselves as they want. Community members can text into the group by knowing the school code, and they manage their own Remind settings.
- Flexible Messaging: School leaders can provide personalized messages to various groups, larger classes, or individuals.
- Safe: With Remind, the phone number of school leaders is kept confidential and is never shared. Plus, the same holds true for anyone who joins your Remind group. All phone numbers are completely confidential and are not used for marketing in any way. School leaders can access a history of their messages anytime, and the same can be done for teachers in your school.
- Conversation: Remind makes large group announcements just as easy as communicating to one member of your group.
- Rich Messages: Much like a tweet of 140 characters or less, the messages that can be sent on Remind include photos, videos, and attachments.
- Schedule Messaging: Messages can be created anytime and scheduled to go out at a specified time. Plus, school leaders can set office hours and only receive messages during these designated times.
- World Languages: All Remind messages can be translated into over 70 languages to engage community members regardless of their language.
- Collaboration: Increase the use of your Remind group/class by adding owners to your group. This allows other leaders within your institution to have control of your Remind groups.
- Office Hours: This shows students and parents when teachers and administrators are available for messaging. If people choose to send messages outside of the office hours, school leaders will still receive them.

Future focused school leaders use communication in a creative, innovative, and relational manner to engage all members of the school community. They understand that if they are not telling their school's story, someone else will. Communication needs to be intentional for school leaders but they can't do this alone. The most effective school leaders understand the importance of collaborating with teachers, students, and parents to communicate their school's mission to the larger school community. They know how to expand their messaging by encouraging others to participate in the communication, collaborate for creative ways to message, and identify key areas of the school life to showcase. Typically, the areas to showcase include student learning, student work, student and teacher testimonies, celebrations of individual and school achievements, and school events. A constant reminder to school leaders is to expand their audience beyond students, teachers, and parents into other community members such as realtors, businesses, clergy, and senior citizens. By doing this, the school leader develops a wider range of buy-in for the school and school life.

Browse the resources at our website, and the Resources Section of this book, for a Communication Plan template school leaders can use to frame their communication in a way that considers key points to engage the school community.

School Leader's Story
Communicating by Relating

Leaders:	David Raft and Theresa Stager
School:	Saline High School
Website:	http://salineschools.org/schools/saline-high-school/
Setting:	Suburban
Size:	1,773 students
Grades:	9–12
Population:	90% white, 5% Asian, 2% African American, 2% Hispanic, 1% multiracial
Poverty:	8% economically disadvantaged
District:	Saline Area Schools
Location:	Saline, MI

Photo courtesy of David Raft

Photo courtesy of Theresa Stager

David Raft graduated from Saline Area Schools and remained as an educator in the same district for almost 20 years, serving as administrator for a large number of those years. This is his first year as principal at Saline High School, the first building he worked in when he became a teacher in the district. Theresa Stager is in her first year at Saline High School as assistant principal. She spent eight years teaching K–12 music and then was principal for three years at a K–8 Catholic school. Raft and Stager are working together for the first time, but they share many of the same philosophies on connecting with their school communities.

The first step to being able to genuinely communicate with your staff, students, parents, and community is building authentic relationships with each of these groups. Saline has 1,773 students, and each student has different beliefs, hobbies, thoughts, families, and goals. Of course it will take quite a while to meet each and every one and make a legitimate connection with them, but this is where your communication must begin. Raft and Stager have spent their careers getting to know as many students as possible by interacting with as many of them as possible—working in classrooms and participating in discussions while in them, greeting each student in the hallway in the morning, and becoming a part of the clubs in the building. By creating a culture of connecting with students, they ensure that students feel they can approach administration about anything; this makes every part of the job a little less complicated and much more meaningful.

Each morning, after greeting students in the hallways, Stager and Raft stop in to classrooms just to say hello. Connecting on a personal level with staff makes the workplace environment a much more pleasant and collaborative one. Staff members feel valued when you stop in, see a lesson or project they have been working on, and involve yourself in it while you're there. Each day, Raft makes sure the entire high school administrative staff is out of their offices, interacting in classes and making sure to visit teachers they have not spent a lot of time around yet in the year. To help this process, administrative offices are intentionally located throughout the building, not just in the Main Office. Stager's office used to be an "end cap" of a hallway, but it's been turned into an office. Her location is amazing for relationship building. Teachers and students are in and out all day, walking by, smiling, saying hello, and connecting.

By getting to know the families in Saline, Raft learns what they are passionate about. This enables him to create opportunities and get them involved in the school. The school asks for volunteers to share their time and talents within the building as well as opportunities for students to learn out in the community.

The Foundation for Saline Area Schools is a group that's looking to give back to their schools. Alumni and local businesses offer scholarships for students to pursue their passions after high school. Because state funding in Michigan has decreased in the last 10 years, a lot of funding for the arts, some sports, classroom grants, and more now comes from the generosity of our foundation, alumni, and local businesses.

School leaders embrace the foundation's yearly events because they further the financial and academic goals of the district. The foundation provides fantastic opportunities for students to interact with our community.

Key Chapter Takeaways

Future focused school leaders realize communication builds community! When community is developed and nurtured, the school benefits through the fertile soil of collaboration and increased learning opportunities for all students. Students gain authentic audiences for their learning, educators win the support of community members, and school leaders earn the confidence and trust of their whole community. True learning is relational, and increased communication fosters a spirit of community engagement for all in the school community. Social media can be a big part of community building when its use is regular, frequent, relational, and focused. When school leaders use social media in this manner, the community gets engaged, your school is strengthened, and parents are more confident in you as a leader. The school is telling its own story.

RELATE, INNOVATE, INVIGORATE ACTIVITIES

Relate

- Create a Remind group and begin to send out messages that require participants to respond to the message.
- Write a principal blog to share a learning dialogue with your school community.
- Create a communication plan in collaboration with faculty, staff, and students.

Innovate

- Hold a Twitter Takeover Day by a student or educator. Train them together and follow the guidelines provided in the Resources Section of the book to lead the Twitter Takeover.
- Post one live video feed on social media from your school this week.
- Create an online Smore newsletter and share it with your school community and realtors, businesses, and beyond.

Invigorate

- Create a Remind group with your faculty/staff and use it to send out positive notes of encouragement. Hide donuts somewhere in the building and send the directions out via a Remind message— this helps increase participation. Or send out a message allowing the faculty/staff to cut out early one day when possible.

- Make a Wordle using reflections from students, staff, faculty, and parents on what is the best thing about your school. Turn the Wordle into a social media post and share it out.
- Create a video of your students and staff that best represents your school's core values and mission.

Team Talk: Relate

Work with your school leadership team to host a Facebook Live or YouTube Live session for parents or students in your school. Identify the topic, market the event, and host the live event as a school leadership team. We would love to share your work with other school leaders, so be sure to post a link at **www.chaselearning.org/TeamTalk**.

Continue the conversation with us on Twitter at #chaselearning.

Connecting to Make a Difference

Building Relationships With the Entire School Community

"Education is the most powerful weapon which you can use to change the world."

—Nelson Mandela

*T*his chapter tells the stories of schools that are building relationships with the entire school community and making a difference because of the engagement and partnerships they create and nurture. Analysis of successes will include practical applications for other settings. We will remind leaders of the calling that brought them to the role of educational leadership, and the great need to reach all students with a relevant education for our changing world. These partnerships include, but are not limited to, partnerships with businesses, community groups, and other service educational agencies within their own community. Plus, we will highlight schools that are serving their community, principals that are making a true difference with their students, and how school leaders can serve not just their students but the entire school community. Funding in education is in peril, and schools are scrambling to find ways to fund projects and meet simple needs; we will give principals tools to attain funding for their schools and creative ideas to leverage resources to help their schools and students find success. Everyone benefits when our schools are strong, and this chapter will help leaders engage the partners needed for true success.

School Leader's Story
Connecting Students With Their Community

Leader: Chaerea Denning-Snorton

School: Nashville Big Picture High School

Website: http://schools.mnps.org/ nashville-big-picture-high-school/

Setting: Urban

Size: 182 students

Grades: 9–12

Population: 56% white, 34% black, 9% Hispanic, 1% Asian

Poverty: 59% economically disadvantaged

District: Metro Nashville Public Schools

Location: Nashville, TN

Photo courtesy of Chaerea Denning-Snorton

Nashville Big Picture High School (BPHS) is the first Big Picture Learning Network School in the south. The Big Picture model is a 20-year-old national movement that has "Ten Distinguishers" to frame the learning. They include focusing on one student at a time, using an advisory structure, authentic assessment, leadership, post-secondary planning, and so on. Two other distinguishers are prominently in play at Nashville BPHS: learning through interests and internships (LTIs), and engaging parents and community.

Students at Nashville Big Picture High School must meet the same requirements for graduation as all other Metro Nashville Public Schools (MNPS) high schools. Beyond those requirements, every student must have an internship in his or her area of interest, attended by students on Tuesdays and Thursdays. Students also complete quarterly exhibitions with parent meetings (required parent attendance) that follow to measure student success and to establish goals for students. One-on-one sessions are held with advisors where students are actively invested in their learning and are challenged to pursue their interests by a supportive community of educators, professionals, and family members.

Each Monday, Wednesday, and Friday students experience workshops and participate in content learning during the morning followed by independent work time in the afternoon. On Tuesday and Thursday students attend informational interviews, job shadow experiences, community service activities, or internships based on their career interests and passions. Dual-enrollment students who attend Nashville State Community College or Tennessee College of Applied Technology may have classes at varying times during the week.

Over 30 community partnerships are listed on their website. Listed partners include: The Parthenon, Essence Day Spa, Saint Thomas Hospital, Provence Breads & Cafe, Pet Resorts of America, Cupcake Collection, West Nashville Law Offices, Goldthreate Tennis, Hatcher and Fell Photography, and Vanderbilt University. Chaerea Denning-Snorton and her staff use nine key steps in their internship model to help students find their interests and establish relationships with their mentors.

She adds, "It is an honor to assist students, parents and staff as we all explore the importance of student guided learning including real-world experiences. Having community stakeholders to serve as mentors for our students has been a major caveat in the success of our school and in the lives of our students. Weekly our mentors tirelessly provide guidance and support to their mentees and the mentees in return learn personal responsibility and the inner workings of area businesses. Students walk away equipped with increased 21st century skills which assist them in being college and career ready."

As Denning-Snorton reflects on the process, she recounts, "I can recall stories of students being overwhelmed with nervousness as they began the internship process including researching career fields. Our staff and our students reassure one another that they could successfully complete the call, the interview and obtain an internship. This year we have over 130 mentors for our students. It is astonishing as one sees the vision of our students' 'Big Picture' becoming a reality."

You can learn more about the success of Nashville Big Picture High School on the Edutopia website. Nashville BPHS is featured in Edutopia's Schools That Work segments online that can be viewed at www .edutopia.org.

CONNECTING FOR LEARNING

The days of schools being isolated castles are gone! Schools and school leaders need to widen their reach and expand to broaden the opportunities for students. School leaders need to be active in the community to make a true and sustaining difference for students. We need to rise up and work to make connections in the community, region, and world. These connections should be centrally focused to provide strengthened learning opportunities for students, to serve the community, and to identify creative funding to widen learning for all students.

I'd like you to think of school leaders as connectors, entrepreneurs, and community leaders. We need to be connecting our school to the community and world, and working to find alternative funding streams. More than ever, our communities and world need school leaders who are willing to think differently in regard to how we do school leadership. This chapter will focus on the school leader's role of connecting to make a difference for their students and community.

SCHOOL, IT'S NOT JUST FOR STUDENTS ANYMORE

Throughout this book, you will hear how passionate we are about educating every child in a highly relational, invigorating, innovative, and inspiring learning environment. We believe that regardless of a child's race, ethnicity, socioeconomic status, religion, or sexual orientation it's our sole responsibility to love, care for, educate, and teach these students to do amazing things in this present world and in the future. To do this, schools need to consider reaching beyond the lives of students. When we support, care for, and educate parents, grandparents, and guardians, the lives of our students improve. Plus, when we model what it means to serve our community, our students and faculty embrace this core value and model it in their own lives. Oftentimes, schools are centerpieces in the community, not just geographically, but also in terms of resources, employment, and service. This provides school leaders with the leverage to truly make a difference for their students and the entire community. They can become the wellspring of life for many members of the community, providing hope, education, resources, and opportunities that strengthen learning for all students.

For this to be accomplished, school leaders need to see themselves as more than simply a building leader or manager but as one who can work to shape, or more accurately, reshape the culture in a community. As school leaders, we can work to grow, encourage, serve, educate, teach, protect, help, and bless a community. This transcends the understanding of many school leaders who see their responsibilities ending at the boundaries of their school. But, to make true transformational change and to model future focused leadership, school leaders need to extend their influence, expertise, and focus beyond the schoolhouse doors.

Here are some key strategies that every school leader should consider to strengthen business and community partnerships.

- Focus on Community Involvement: This may sound simple, but so often school leaders can get consumed with what's going on in the school that they are overwhelmed to extend their reach beyond the school. Getting into the community means visiting businesses and community organizations and introducing yourself, give your contact information, and ask how the school can partner with them.

- Focus on People: Be intentional at meeting and connecting with business leaders. You can do this by joining your local Chamber of Commerce, joining local organizations like the Rotary or Lions Club, or in visiting a church, mosque, or temple in your community. Work to make connections with key members in your community and make sure these relationships are two-way supporting systems. Don't relate just to take, but be sure to support and give back to these relationships.

- Focus on Supporting Law Enforcement/Emergency Management/ Medical Professionals: These great leaders can provide rich and powerful resources for your students, staff, and parents. Strong partnerships with these groups are mission critical, not just when you need their help but on a regular basis to make strong connections in the community.

- Focus on Service: How can you serve in your school community? Whether it's being a volunteer umpire, serving on a board of a nonprofit, or simply helping out at community events, there's nothing better to strengthen community partnerships than volunteering.

Below are some ways that schools can serve their community and beyond. These are only a few examples—we would love to hear what you are doing that's making a difference in your community. Please be sure to share your story with us by going to our website so we can feature your story.

Digital Tools for All

Community Makerspaces: The popularity of Makerspaces is sweeping across the country, but there are many communities and schools that cannot afford the technology that many Makerspaces have. This is where a school can partner with their community to foster collaboration around designing, innovation, and creativity. If your school has a Makerspace that includes 3D printers, laser cutters, and more, invite the community to use this resource—or perhaps schools can partner with a business, industry, or Makerspace in their area. Come together to enrich resources for students and faculty.

Mobile Tech Help Center: This is one area that could really blossom in schools. Train students and staff to become trouble-shooters with regard to technology. Open up your school as a mobile tech help center for the community. Whether it be fixing the hardware on computers, resolving software issues, or simply training community members on how to use technology, students are often more advanced in this area than community members. I love the Apple Genius Bar in our local Apple Store. It's a place where I know I can go to get high-quality training, tech help, or simply to learn something new. Now I can hear my elementary friends saying, "Yes, but this is such a secondary thing." You would be surprised what elementary students can do in teaching community members about technology. Why not have your elementary students teach a senior citizen community how to use their iPads? During Grandparents' Day have students teach their grandparents how to use their mobile devices in a new and innovative way. Elementary students see life without boundaries or limits—allow them to think creatively on how they can serve as mobile tech help for their community. As school leaders, we need to use the expertise of our students and teach them how to teach others about the great things they are doing. I recently had a student who went and worked on computers in a local community center to clean up viruses, speed up their processing, and update software. The community center director thanked me by sharing how the student was so helpful.

Community Hotspot: Way too many of our students and families lack access to the Internet at home. Again, this is an example of the financial divide that parlays into resources for wealthy students and results in the lack of resources for economically disadvantaged students. Schools that are one-to-one should be providing students and families with mobile hotspots to allow equal access to resources on the Internet. Plus, community members who do not have Wi-Fi access often find it difficult to search for and apply for jobs, find resources to help them advance, and participate in online learning. Schools should consider being hotspots where community members can come to the school to use free Wi-Fi that is fast, easy to use, and reliable. Plus, it's always good when the schools have someone available to show the community member how to get connected and what resources can really help them.

Community Tech Hubs: Schools should be opening their technology to community members. Allow community members to come in and use the school's technology. This can be done after school hours or during school hours if closely supervised. Host special events that focus on using technology for such things as applying for college or a job, filing their taxes online, looking for scholarships for their kids, creative couponing to save money, and how to budget online.

Learning and Growing Together

GED Classes: Perhaps one of the greatest things that a school leader can do is to equip their students' parents with the tools to access higher levels of education. With this purpose in mind, I decided to teach a GED course for free to community members. I worked with community and school members to find funding for the adults to take their GED exam and get them the proper study guides. A great blessing was to celebrate with one of my GED students when they passed; we got a cap and gown, and honored them in front of their spouse and children. You see, when a parent grows in learning and education, the student excels in the classroom and beyond. Work with your faculty to provide a free GED course for your school community. This is how you bring about true transformational change that is sustainable and meaningful. After the GED class, help these adults apply to the local community college or work with them to fill out job applications. It's about coming alongside these GED students and being there for them. In partnership with the community center director, we worked to provide transportation to the testing center, bought the needed supplies, and even provided child care. If we are going to really talk about making real change for our students, we need to strengthen the level of education in their homes.

Community Garden: I love the power of gardening; it provides students and the community a chance to partner to find true joy and the fruits of their labor. Consider hosting a community garden that is cared for by your students and community members. Give the crops away to a local homeless shelter, the Salvation Army, or any community agency that provides for those in need. Or, host a community dinner between students and community members to enjoy the fresh veggies. Community gardens are easy to get funded through companies such as Lowe's, Home Depot, Walmart, or Target. These companies will regularly donate plants and other gardening supplies. Plus, they may even lend employees to help build, plant, and maintain the garden.

Use these community garden experiences for students to produce writing pieces, pictures, video documentaries, or other products. Use this student created work to tell the story to a wider audience and build participation and support. Consider reading *Seedfolks*, written by Paul Fleischman and illustrated by Judy Pedersen, as a "one book, one community" event. This book brings powerful lessons in diversity education in the context of a garden. There are countless ways to engage schools and community members; it's important that school leaders continue to search for avenues to build partnerships between the school and community. When this is done, students benefit and learn great things that go beyond the classroom.

School Leader's Story
Engaging the Community

Leader: Devin Padavil

School: Lebanon Trail High School

Website: http://schools.friscoisd.org/hs/lebanontrail

Setting: Suburban

Size: 500 students (projection is 2,000 students in 2020)

Grades: 9–12 (this new school opened with 9th grade only in 2016–17)

Population: 40% white, 32% Asian, 18% African American, 10% Hispanic

Poverty: 15% economically disadvantaged

District: Frisco Independent School District

Location: Frisco, TX

Photo courtesy of Devin Padavil

This excerpt is written by school leader Devin Padavil:

"A strategy we used at Lebanon Trail High School involved engaging the community and staff to build a Graduate Profile. Essentially, we asked the question 'What are your highest aspirations for a four-year graduate of LTHS?' While the process led to a product, the greatest benefit of this process was the strengthening of relationship between parents, community members, and staff members. Each stakeholder bonded around a common vision for the type of school they were being asked to help create. Using a process to organize the input of all included, we developed four over-arching themes:

- Future Focused Leadership
- Innovation
- Socially Responsible
- Internally Driven by Values

These goals helped us refine a vision and mission for our school. The vision, mission, and graduate profile process can be viewed online at: https://lthspride.com/2016/05/02/lths-graduate-profile/.

More importantly, our teachers use the graduate profile to help students establish short-term and long-term goals for the school year. In this way, the graduate profile is a tool that helps to invigorate teachers and students toward greater self-development and achievement.

Innovation is a core value that can be seen on the walls of many schools. However, many schools fall short of innovation when they lack goals and a vision. The graduate profile process at LTHS is an example of inspiring authentic innovation among teams and individuals in a school fulfilling their vision and mission."

PARTNERSHIPS TO STRENGTHEN LEARNING

I absolutely loved what I observed while visiting Shenzhen, China, and the STEM Education Foundation. I learned from the directors, engineers by trade, that they possessed a passion to educate children living in some of the poorest and most remote areas of China. The mission of the STEM Education Foundation is "to improve teacher quality of elementary and secondary schools in remote and poor regions around the world, and to share quality educational resources, allowing more children around the world to receive a sound modern education" (STEM Education Foundation, n.d.).

Photo courtesy of Shenzhen, China - STEM Education Foundation

I was inspired by Harrison Xia, the secretary-general of the STEM Educational Foundation, as he shared the vision and mission of this organization. He spoke passionately about the Foundation's effort to provide every child access to a high quality education as provided to the students in China's metropolitan areas. He said, "Knowledge changes and technology brings reality to dreams." The goal of the STEM Foundation through the use of satellite technology is to create 600,000 classrooms for unattended children from poverty-stricken families living in remote areas of China.

During a tour of the many satellite dishes that are used to send the teaching lessons to remote areas, Xia showcased the technology while explaining how it transmitted those lessons to millions of students throughout the country. He went on to share how the STEM Education

Foundation is working to build a global system that will provide education through advanced broadband satellites, mobile Internet technology, and the establishment of distance education networks in Africa, the Middle East, Southeast Asia, and beyond. The goal is to reach millions of students and to provide them with quality instruction equal to their peers who live in cities such as Shanghai and Shenzhen. The STEM Education Foundation is a shining example of how businesses can partner with schools to provide students with rich learning opportunities for all students. I applaud the innovative engineers and business leaders for their creative effort to educate students throughout the world.

Extending Learning

Because schools need to be more competitive than ever, school leaders need to work to find extensions to the learning for all students. Whether your school is in a rural, suburban, or urban area, school leaders need to tap into the community and global resources to strengthen learning opportunities for their students. Businesses can provide schools with rich resources for learning. For example, Facebook recently launched (pun intended) a new initiative to supply Wi-Fi access to underserved areas around the globe through the use of solar-powered drones that supply wireless access points.

Facebook's Aquila drone, which at cruising speed uses the same wattage as three hairdryers, uses lasers to beam the Internet to remote regions of the Earth. Their first test flights have been successful and the drone will eventually stay airborne continuously for three months. Facebook intends Aquila to be part of a fleet of planes that will provide the Internet to 4 billion people in sub-Saharan Africa and other remote regions that do not have access currently. Jay Parikh, Facebook's head of engineering and infrastructure, said in a blog: "We're encouraged by this first successful flight, but we have a lot of work ahead of us. . . . In our next tests, we will fly Aquila faster, higher and longer, eventually taking it above 60,000 feet" (Farrell, 2016). This may be an extreme example, but do not underestimate the solutions that can be generated when corporations work with schools. These partnerships can produce powerful results that benefit our students and our communities.

Experts

In our local area, scientists from several major pharmaceutical companies provide partnerships with school districts in a number of ways. North Penn School District has science summer camps for students where local scientists volunteer their time. Many will visit the schools throughout the year to give feedback on student projects or highlight application aspects of students' science curriculum in their current work. Lehigh University allows schools to send samples to examine under their electron microscope. The university will send detailed images that go well beyond any microscopes available in the school district. They also connect with classrooms through video conferencing to discuss projects with students. Drexel University has provided engineering professors to collaborate with classes through video conference as well. They have volunteered their time to assist with science projects, and frequently support students pursuing solutions to robotic challenges.

Undoubtedly you have companies, colleges, or universities to invite into a partnership with your school. Many companies want to serve their local communities in this way, and universities often benefit in their grant writing when they can partner with K–12 institutions. If you don't have these relationships, make a few phone calls or e-mail inquiries to see if these resources are available for your students.

Creative Funding for Learning

Too often, the dreams and visions of school leaders die from lack of funding. Funding in education is constantly scrutinized, and school leaders need to get creative in order to provide innovative learning opportunities that have strong funding sources and ongoing support from the community. In this section, we are going to share some powerful resources that school leaders can use to set free the boundless dreams and ideas of their teachers and students. No longer do we need to think about funding before dreaming; now we can dream and then get those dreams funded. It's important to note that this funding piece is aligned with the Relate section of this book. Funding is all about relationships and communication. We need to build business partnerships and learn how to communicate our visions, mission, dreams, and projects to those with the resources to support them.

Business Partnerships

More than just money, businesses can provide countless resources such as school supplies, technology, and personnel. So many businesses are outstanding at this. There are literally thousands of businesses worldwide that support education. For example, Walmart provides millions of dollars each year to local schools right in their community. Their local grants work to fund projects that teachers, students, and school leaders have initiated to support students in their school. They regularly provide schools with resources such as school supplies, garden supplies, and food. Many of my colleagues in school leadership share with me all that their school has received from Walmart. I tell you this, because it's all about tapping into the resources right in your backyard. Big corporate companies can be more difficult to get funding from; however, local and community-based businesses are often more than willing to provide support to their local school. This is even more true when they have a connection to your school, a project that they can get excited about, or a school leader that has worked to establish a strong relationship with them. A hint for you when going for a corporate grant or funding: Many corporations are beginning to shy off of just funding technology such as iPads for a class. However, they get very excited about passion projects that show growth, inspiration stories, and examples of things that are making real change in the lives of students.

The Fairy Grantmother

Dacia Jones serves as the district science specialist and STEM educator for Durham Public Schools in Durham, North Carolina. We had the opportunity to attend one of her professional development sessions at a Discovery Education event. In addition to her passion for science and STEM education, Jones is dedicated to helping all students access the resources and opportunities needed for a relevant, authentic, and technology-immersed experience. She says, "Finding ways to get what we need in the classroom has never been easier. Learn the secrets to getting your grants funded quickly." Many of her tips relate to using national chains in your local area, in addition to larger grant writing opportunities. Her session was inspiring, and eye opening. Many businesses are seeking partnerships with schools and classrooms, and we may be missing the chance to partner with them.

Workplace Giving Programs

Lowe's, Target, State Farm, Best Buy, Wells Fargo, and other corporations have specific grant opportunities for public and nonpublic schools. A quick web search will get you to their specific programs and opportunities. Many corporations will allow employees to match funds, volunteer time, provide teams, match your fundraising, or provide other monies and services. Double the Donation (2016) is a site that consolidates resources through workplace giving online for nonprofits. While this site highlights national and international businesses, don't overlook similar programs going on in your area. For example, we have received funds for robotics and engineering-related curriculum from a local engineering firm for several years.

Donors Choose (www.DonorsChoose.org) is a website that funds dreams in schools. This is one of the easiest and best ways to fund school programs. A school leader can simply post a school project they want to get funded and Donors Choose find donors to support the request. School leaders can watch their projects get funded.

School Leader's Story
Making a Difference for Others

Leader:	Mark Mayer
School:	Talley Middle School
Website:	http://www.brandywineschools.org/talley
Setting:	Urban
Size:	752 students
Grades:	6–8
Population:	41.2% white, 41.0% black, 8.4% Asian, 7.6% Hispanic, 1.8% multiracial
Poverty:	40% economically disadvantaged
District:	Brandywine School District
Location:	Wilmington, DE

Photo courtesy of Mark Mayer

The first thing I saw when I walked in the door of Talley Middle School was a banner that read, "At 211 degrees, water is hot. At 212 degrees, it boils. And with boiling water, comes steam. And with steam, you can power a train. One extra degree makes all the difference." School leader Mark Mayer and his amazing faculty and staff are committed to teaching students that they are the one degree that makes a difference in their community. Each year, his school selects a nonprofit to support through fund raising, student contributions, and partnerships. The focus of the entire school year is how Talley Middle School can be that one degree that powers the nonprofit organization to the next level. Most recently, the school selected the Ronald McDonald House, a temporary home for families with children in the Children's Hospital who are battling cancer and other traumas. Talley students contributed their artwork, volunteered with this organization, and raised funds to support families who have ill children in the home. Throughout the entire school year, students raise money through school dances, competitions, and various fund-raisers. But it's more than just giving their money; students learn to give back to their community and the power of volunteering. Various musical groups perform and bring

(Continued)

(Continued)

cheer to those staying at the Ronald McDonald House, and students volunteer encouragement and inspiration to families going through unthinkably hard times. This year, Talley selected a local autistic foundation to support. Talley students will be learning about autism, working with students who have autism, and supporting the foundation through their generous fundraising. Just like Talley, your school can pick up real steam in teaching students the value of giving back to their community and making a real difference by transforming the world into a better place. Mayer reflects, "We strive to establish real relationships that have real significance, which will lead to meaningful lives that will serve others!"

Key Chapter Takeaways

What got you excited about school leadership? For us it was the notion of creating a space where all students and staff could create a strong community—like the communities we built in our classrooms. In this setting *all* students can find success. Schools will be most successful when they build partnerships beyond their own school walls. The reasons to make connections are focused in three areas: to provide strengthened learning opportunities for students, to serve the community, and to identify creative funding to widen learning for all students.

STEM and STEAM learning opportunities provide a great avenue to invite parents, university professors, local engineers, designers, and others working in these fields to connect more intentionally with your school. Leverage your service organizations, like National Honor Society, National Junior Honor Society, student government, community helpers, Makerspaces, or service learning requirements, to build connections and support your community. Build your alternate funding network to generate opportunities for your students and staff. In many ways the success of your community connections as a school will be directly connected to your successful connecting as the school leader.

RELATE, INNOVATE, INVIGORATE ACTIVITIES

Relate

- Attend a local Rotary, Lions Club, or Chamber of Commerce meeting to talk about the things going on at your school. Build relationships with community business leaders.

- Contact a local college/university and invite engineering and computer science professors to support robotics or coding activities with your students.
- Find out if your local community college will support your students with a homework help line after school. You get extended support and they begin to build relationships with prospective students.

Innovate

- Spend time at a faculty meeting discussing the possibilities that follow a grant funding success by posing the hypothetical question, "What will we do with the $15,000 we're awarded for our students, school, and community?"
- Pose the same audacious question to your students and compare their answers to the suggestions generated by the professional staff.
- Apply to fund a school project through Donors Choose.

Invigorate

- Share a story from a school that received grant funding and did something amazing for their students and community to get your professional staff excited about dreaming big. Work with them to generate an "impossible" idea that could be accomplished with extra funding and partners.
- Contact local businesses and see if they will feature, and sell, student artwork in a partnership like Zoe's Kitchen. This will increase foot traffic to their business, give an authentic audience for student work, and result in extra funds for the school.
- Get your students into the community. Select a nonprofit for your school to adopt similar to Talley Middle School.

Team Talk: Relate

Choose from one of the three below—or do all three! Please share your experience at **www.chaselearning.org/TeamTalk**.

As a school leadership team:

1. Volunteer in your school community—look for ways to give back right in your school community.

2. Host a business luncheon and showcase the work of your students and staff.

3. Identify a project that your students and staff need funding for and work to write a grant using the guidance of the Fairy Grantmother.

Continue the conversation with us on Twitter at #chaselearning.

Shift in How We Do School

The Changing Architecture of Learning and Schooling

"If we teach today's students as we taught yesterday's, we rob them of tomorrow."

—John Dewey

"Nothing could be more absurd than an experiment in which computers are placed in a classroom where nothing else is changed."

—Seymour Papert

This chapter will highlight the habits that hold us back and the changes that can unleash powerful learning. Examples of learning environments beyond the traditional school model will be examined for applications to the leader's own setting. This chapter will examine how school leaders can redesign the physical structure of traditional classrooms and schools to foster innovation, how to extend learning beyond the classroom walls, and how to design learning environments that nurture creativity and innovation. These replicable practices will guide leaders to sustaining innovation in their schools. Our students' learning does not stop when the school bell rings, and we must become relevant learning environments or risk extinction.

School Leader's Story
Increasing Parent Involvement

Leaders:	Susan Higginson and Kyle Crater
School:	Amanda E. Stout Elementary School
Website:	http://www.readingsd.org/amandastout
Setting:	Urban
Size:	900 students
Grades:	K–5
Population:	80.7% Latino, 9.3% black, 6.9% white, 2.5% multiracial, 0.6% Asian; 18.2% English language learners
Poverty:	93.3% economically disadvantaged
District:	Reading School District
Location:	Reading, PA

Photo courtesy of Susan Higginson and Kyle Crater

At Amanda E. Stout Elementary School in Reading School District of Reading, Pennsylvania, the principal team of Susan Higginson and Kyle Crater led their school through student-led conferences. This elementary school is leading with the students at the heart of their work. They are working to think differently in how they do schooling and how they engage students and parents.

Assistant Principal Kyle Crater writes, "The number one challenge for our school is increasing parent involvement. Out of approximately 900 students in grades K–5, we may only see 100 parents on Meet the Teacher Night or during Parent–Teacher Conferences. It's not that parents don't want to be involved in our school; but the demographic of our community is unique when compared to our surrounding school districts. Many of our students come from single-parent homes, foster homes, or the primary guardian is an older sibling or aunt/uncle, or grandmother/grandfather. Plus, the reality that nobody likes to mention is the demographic of our staff is not like the surrounding community. The one piece of common ground that we share, however, is the students, and how much we care for them."

Piloted last school year with several classes, student-led conferences transferred the conversation that takes place with the parent from the teacher to the student. Kyle continues, "The teacher is there as a facilitator and to answer any follow-up questions. This is one component of a Leadership-themed Character Education program that is being implemented schoolwide in the coming school year. The two classes that piloted

Student-Led Conferences reported 100% attendance for all Parent/Teacher Conferences. This was unprecedented to what our school typically experiences. When asked for feedback, most parents commented simply that they wanted to be there due to the fact that it would be their child presenting their academic material to them. They recognized the work that their child had put in to prepare their presentation and wanted to be there to support them. The bottom line, their child is someone that they can relate to during a conversation. Moving forward, all students will have a Leadership Data binder where they will compose a personal mission statement, an academic goal, and a behavioral goal that they wish to accomplish. They will also track their benchmark data so they can be more aware of their gains in relation to their academic goals. This binder will be the template followed for Student-Led Conferences. The students will be able to simply open their binder, talk about their goals, what they've done so far to get there, what challenges they're still experiencing, and how they plan to overcome those challenges. We're excited to see how our entire school community transforms and bonds as we all rally behind our student leaders."

HOLDING BACK INNOVATION: COMFORT, COST, AND COURAGE

Innovation is often held back, for school leaders, by simple things such as the use of cell phones, dress codes, recess, lunch monitoring, bus duty, and so many other things that come flying into the daily work of a school leader. A school leader can frequently be distracted by teacher complaints, and as soon as one fire is put out another one erupts. It can easily be cell phones, dress code violations, hallway distractions, students not dressing for physical education, or not enough proctors for recess duty. Although these are key activities that school leaders need to take care of, it must not extinguish the creative, innovative, and discovery focus of the leader and their team. Take time to establish clear procedures for these distractors and trust others to intervene on your behalf. Don't ignore them, but don't focus on them because "What You Focus on Grows!" Getting out of the rut isn't easy, but it is necessary to be an innovative leader.

You don't need to wait until you come up with the next greatest idea or the hottest program for schools—act now, take a step forward, and walk out of the rut. Rarely do educators like change, and as a result, we can be unintentionally led into a rut by well-meaning educators who are clinging to the status quo out of habit or simply out of fear of moving beyond their own comfort zones. Rise above the distractions, be courageous, and lead with boldness. The key is to focus on what you want to grow. Below are some distractors that can pull us away from innovation and into the rut. I call these distractors the Three Cs; once you work through these Three Cs, you can see the true lens for innovation in your school.

- Comfort: Innovation is not comfortable because it requires failure, risks, and resilience. School leaders are regularly swayed by their own comforts and attracted to the familiar. Whether it's a routine, a common practice, or a tradition, school leaders can be tied to these things even if they hinder movement toward innovation. We can often cling to the past out of comfort and fear of rocking the boat. Innovation is like losing weight—it's something we all talk about and want to do, but regularly fail in making the commitment to move away from our regular eating habits to elicit the true change that we dream about. Here are some practical strategies to reawaken your focus toward innovation:
  - Read: This sounds so cliché, but reading is a powerful way to stretch your thinking and expand your horizon toward innovation.
  - Listen: Podcasts can be a boost of energy to take the next step in innovation. Listen to the various school leaders who are doing great things toward innovation. Check out the list of possible podcasts at the end of the chapter.
  - View: Whether it be a TED Talk, a YouTube video, or a short inspirational video clip, watching videos can open up one's eyes to new ideas, concepts, and ways of doing things.
  - Connect: Without a doubt, we grow the most from connecting with other school leaders and dreaming about how we can redo schooling.

- Cost: So many school leaders make excuses that they don't have the funds to innovate. Innovation does not need to break your school's budget. Innovation on a shoestring is possible and actually taking place in many schools around the country. Cost can also be much more than money. School leaders are fearful to innovate at the cost of test scores and achievement on standardized assessments. To really prepare students for the future, we can't rely on test scores but creativity, communication, teamwork, collaboration, and innovation. Here are some ways to fund your innovative ideas:
  - Donations: You would be surprised what your school community has laying around that they would love to get rid of. These donations, from businesses, churches, parents, and community members, can innovate with little out-of-pocket expenses.

○ Grants: There are grants that often go untapped by school leaders. For example, I just a found a national business that has a local work site near my school and gives grants to schools for rain gardens. After talking with the company, my school is going to receive a free rain garden for our students to use.

○ Business Partnerships: It's important that you are working with your local businesses to share your ideas and dreams for your school. If your school can't afford a 3D printer, why don't you check around to see if a business has a 3D printer that would allow your school to use it after hours. Or, ask a business to sponsor your Makerspace—allow them to have naming rights to your creative location.

○ Donors Choose (www.donorschoose.org): This website lets you post a financial need for your classroom or school and receive funding from participants. It's a Kickstarter-style site for teachers and schools.

• Courage: You've heard it said that failure is not an option, but failure is not only an option with innovation, it's almost a certainty. School leaders need to embrace failure. Innovation can be messy and dirty, but this can't stop us from our focus to make real change for students. Students need visionary leaders who are willing to boldly lead their school into the future. This type of leadership takes courage! Not the type of courage to jump out of an airplane skydiving for the first time or the nerve-wracking adventure of white-water rafting, but the courage to stand for what is right, to admit you aren't the smartest person in the room, to be vulnerable to ask for help, and to learn about something that you know nothing about. Work to garner courage by doing the following:

○ Mission: Return to the core mission of being an educator and to make a difference in the lives of students.

○ Student Centered: Schedule meetings with students with the sole purpose of having them teach you something new. It could be a new pop song, a drone creation, or how to use our MakerBot.

○ Collaborative: It's easier to be courageous when you have people around you who you can dream with and vision cast for your students.

"I model innovation and reflect on things when they don't work out. I work to try and review, but my staff never sees me give up." – Dr. Senée Bell, school leader at Morton Ranch Junior High School.

Finally, consider the courage focus in the words of the Reverend Billy Graham: "Courage is contagious. When a brave man takes a stand, the spines of others are often stiffened." Take a stand for your students today and you will be surprised how others come around you. People are just waiting on you to be courageous!

A FUTURE CRISIS: PULLING AWAY FROM THE PAST TO SAVE THE FUTURE

Every 26 seconds, a student drops out of school, and 25% of all high school freshmen fail to graduate on time or at all. Sadly, high school dropouts commit about 75% of the crimes in this nation (DoSomething.org, n.d.). Schools are thirsty for real innovation that rethinks how we do school. Our country is hungry for schools that are not preparing students for prison but for the workplace, college, and beyond.

For school leaders, your future started yesterday so get ready to embrace the change that is needed to truly innovate in your school. Schools look very similar to the time when our dad, grandfather, and great grandfather went to school. Most schools still have students sitting in rows, moving to class at the sound of a bell, and having the teacher as the only evaluator of their work.

Unleash Powerful Learning

Which country do you think has the most Nobel Prize winners? If you guessed China, Finland, Singapore, the United Kingdom, or India you are incorrect. The most winners come from the United States. To date, there are 356 Nobel Prize winners from the United States but China has only nine. That's right, nine Nobel Peace Prize winners. What does that tell us about our country? It highlights the importance of the entrepreneurial spirit, creativity, innovation, our endless discovery, and a focus on improving life through inventions and new designs.

Our schools need to have this same type of innovation, creativity, discovery, and entrepreneurial spirit as our 356 Nobel Prize winners. We can learn a great deal from them. In this portion of the chapter you will hear directly from school leaders who are innovating in their schools for student success. You will learn practical strategies you can immediately and thoughtfully implement in your school. We're going to shoot straight with you—some of these strategies are easy to execute and some will really stretch your comfort level, but they are all worthwhile and will reinvigorate you and your school to make a sustaining difference for students and your entire community.

Figure 4.1 Future Focused Education

	1900	Now	Future Focused
Teacher	Source of knowledge	Deliverer of knowledge	Facilitator to help students turn knowledge into solutions—innovative inquirer; recruits other experts to help
Student	Work produced for the teacher	Work shared with one or more teachers	Work produced for authentic audiences around the world
Seating	Students seated in rows	Students seated in rows and clusters	Students in groups; mobile, dynamic, and joining from virtual locations
Learning	Learning focused on rote memorization to meet the learning needs of the school	Learning focused on memorization and application to meet the learning needs of the class	Learning focused on personalization to meet the learning needs of each student
Schedule	Bells alerted the change of class; fixed schedule	Bells alert the change of class; fixed schedule	No bells; flexible schedule to meet the learning and physical needs of students
Curriculum	Textbooks primary source of curriculum	Textbooks primary source of curriculum supplemented by online resources	Curriculum driven by finding and solving real-world problems; online learning, Makerspaces, project-based learning
Courses	Taught at school	Taught at school and online	Choice is key; courses taught at school, online, hybrid, college, iTunes, etc.
Evaluation	Teacher is only evaluator of student work	Teacher is only evaluator of student work	Teacher, students, parents, and the world are evaluators of student work
Assessment	Teacher administered with end goal to see if students retained information; goal is ranking students	Administered by teacher, District, and state/federal to assess content retention, standards, and college placement; goal is ranking students and schools	Authentic assessments, administered by teachers, business leaders, and experts, test students' ability to apply learning to new problems; goal is student learning

(Continued)

Figure 4.1 (Continued)

	1900	Now	Future Focused
Course Content	Taken from textbook	Taken from textbooks and websites	Student driven, many choices; created through career readiness and authentic problem solving for the community/world
Technology	Paper and pencil	High-powered computers, handheld devices, wireless access, and mobile technology; we learn about technology	Invisible, ubiquitous, powerful; we learn to learn, using technology

Put the Students in Charge!

Much like the school profile of Winston Sakurai, Hawaii's 2016 Principal of the Year, who had the students design Founder's Hall, you should rely on your students to dream up and create the change in their school. After all, it is *their school*! Whether you are a K–2 school or a Grade 10–12 high school, the students are naturally inclined toward creativity. Sadly, schools often suck creativity right out of their students. Let's include students and their creative thinking to drive the real change needed in our schools. Students possess the energy, enthusiasm, creativity, collaboration, and ability to make a sustaining difference in their school, community, and nation. Below are some examples of how school leaders relied on their students to lead the change in schools.

Student-Led Professional Development Have students lead your teachers on professional development. Maybe it's teaching educators about the latest technology, strategies to include all students, or discussion of ideas they have to make their school better. When students and teachers work together and learn together, true systemic change can take place.

Union R-XI School District in Missouri believes that students have the leadership capacity to provide professional development for their faculty and staff. In this district, both middle and high school students plan, organize, and lead professional development opportunities for teachers (Tarte, 2015). These learning opportunities for teachers, led by students, have been some of the most popular professional development throughout the school year. Check out more of their story at http://www.edutopia.org/blog/student-partnership-in-professional-development-justin-tarte.

Student-Led Conferences The days of parent–teacher conferences where the teacher sits behind their desk, reviews the student's grades, and simply asks the parents if they have any questions need to be updated. Students need to be an integral part of their learning, progress, and conferences. Remember how it changed Amanda E. Stout Elementary School? Here's another example.

Middle School Grades 4–8, C. L. Jones Middle School, Minden School District, Minden, NE

Photo courtesy of John Osgood

School leader John Osgood and his teaching staff host student-led conferences every school year. In the fall, the traditional parent–teacher conference is held but in the spring, students lead the parent conferences. Students have a series of instruments that are put together for them to work on. These include a grade sheet and examples of their work. They choose two items and the teacher picks two items to reflect the quality of student work. The students do a self-assessment on how they feel about the class, their abilities in the class, and how they are doing in the class, and the teachers add to the assessment on how the student is doing on the same page so the parent can see both reflections. They also work on social structures where the students build a coat of arms that identifies them as a student, who their friends are, interests, things they like to do in school and out of school, and the students develop a script on what to do during the parent conference. Since they attend a one-to-one school with iPads, the students are beginning to move all of this work into a digital portfolio and the goal is to have students present their portfolio using the iPad with parents. The students also set academic goals for the year, and they measure that goal to check on their progress. The conference sessions are set up in the classrooms so there are typically about four or five conferences going on in the same room. There is a gap between the conferences to meet the teacher and to get more information from the teacher, and the teacher meets up with the student and the parents to triangulate what the student shared during the student-led conference. Parent turnout for student-led conferences is between 95% and 100%, but it was only 65% to 70% before student-led conferences. Osgood shares, "We have a lot more parents coming into the building and students are accountable for their own learning."

Student Feedback Regularly solicit feedback from students on how to make the school better. Whether it's surveys, small-group feedback meetings, or connecting with a club or sports team, student feedback is critical to develop ownership and support for innovative change. Allow students to respond to open-ended questions about your school with anonymous surveys and they will supply great ideas to improve learning. Schedule student forums weekly to hear from a random group of students and to get feedback on your school.

Try meeting with randomly chosen groups of students, asking them four questions:

What is our school doing great?	What do you dream our school can become?
What can our school improve on?	What can you do to improve the school?

Student Creation Use the creativity of students to move your school toward success. See how one principal turned his school's website over to the students. That's right, students run the school website!

School leader Michael Piccininni, of Coronado High School in Henderson, Nevada (3,300 students), has his students create, run, and keep his school website up to date. The school still has a static and formal web site that is part of the larger district's website, but this student-led website is the life and breath of the school. This is the website that students, parents, teachers, and the entire school community go to for the latest information.

The entire website is student centered and created by students. At Coronado High School, students are responsible for learning coding to create the school website. "We did away with the school newspaper and made this website our online newspaper. It has worked very well; student interest is much higher, and the students are doing the reporting, website design, and taking the lead on it." Students need to attend school and community events to report and design articles that will run on the website. In addition to reporting on special events, students provide updates on important health issues, movie reviews, tips on positive relationships, and so much more. The website is packed with student testimonies, student-created videos, and information about news, sports, media, social media, and an entire section focused on student voice. This student section features an editorial, pro/con, student opinion, and a humor piece that highlights funny things going on in the school and world. Piccininni attributes the success of the website to his teachers and students. "We have amazing students here at Coronado High School who are dedicated to the success of this online newspaper."

PHYSICAL ENVIRONMENT

Many school leaders cannot change the physical structure of their building, but they can change the furniture, classroom setup, use of open spaces, and other areas of the school. We need to move away from having students in rows to a more collaborative model, and we need to consider how to use open areas for student engagement and collaboration.

Classroom redesign is something that all school leaders should consider. Designing the classroom in a manner to enhance engagement is critical. Plus, our learning environments need to mirror the needs and culture of students. Having students in groups at either tables or adjoining desks fosters and nurtures collaboration and team talk with students.

One of the easiest, and cheapest, solutions to creating a more collaborative and engaging physical space is to move desks from rows to clusters of four. Figure 4.2 shows how a classroom with 32 desks can be transformed. This design also allows the teacher to facilitate collaboration and check for understanding by spending time in the "inner circle" and circulating to each group of four. This new arrangement allows for efficient formative assessment by monitoring student talk and connecting to conference with each group. Anywhere you stand in the inner ring places you at close proximity to three groups at once. This physical arrangement allows you to be in the midst of learning while students own the work. The new layout supports the teacher as facilitator of learning.

Open Spaces for Learning and School Furniture That Engages

Use the open spaces in your school for learning and collaboration. Allowing students to use lobbies, hallways, cafeteria spaces, courtyards, and other open areas increases opportunities for collaboration and the collegial environment with students. When we trust students to work in collaborative open spaces a cooperative environment is nurtured. Now I'm not saying to simply release students anywhere in the building without supervision; it's key to set clear expectations, have adult supervision, and establish norms in the building that promote collaboration and respect for learning. More and more, we are seeing school leaders who are using open spaces to create collaborative think tanks where students can write (with washable markers) on glass windows, students can film videos and complete assignments, and students can come together to plan, think, converse, and deliberate over complex issues and learning.

Elementary schools use classroom spaces so well—you almost always see elementary students working collaboratively at tables, work stations,

Figure 4.2 Transforming Learning Environments

Each room pictured here has identical dimensions, but the physical space of desks is significantly improved by changing desks from rows to clusters.

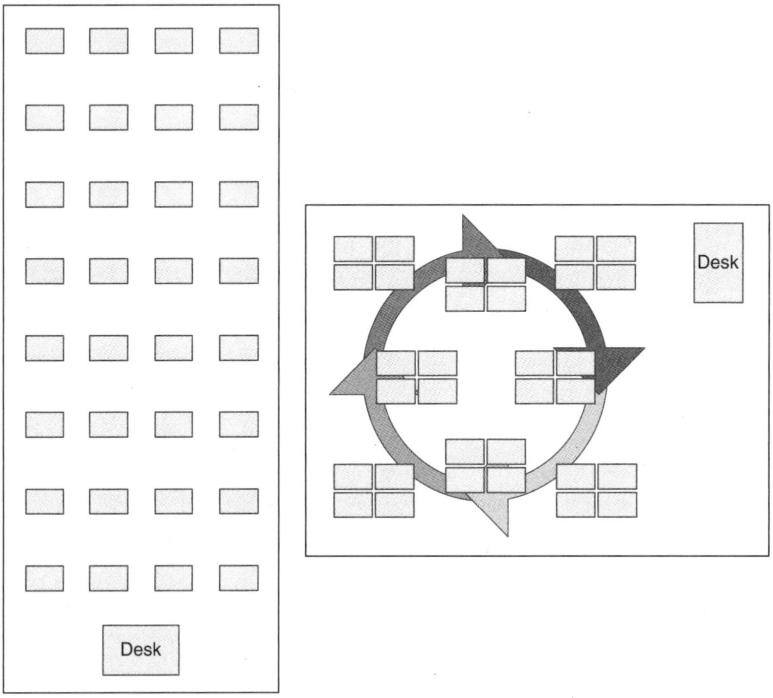

or on the floor. So why is it when students hit the secondary level rows become the norm and collaboration is often stifled by rigid rules and fear of misbehavior. As school leaders, we may have the opportunity to purchase new school furniture for classes and hallways. Use this opportunity to purchase with collaboration in mind.

For example, rather than purchasing traditional desks, go for round tables, boomerang-shaped desks than can easily create groups of three or four, and furniture that allows for a flexible learning environment. Think of high-top round tables that allow students to stand and collaborate like two businesswomen working together at a Starbucks. Why do we always have students seated? In the business world, people are up and moving around, collaborating around standing areas, and many major deals get done in the open spaces of a lobby or coffee area.

We've seen students sitting on exercise ball chairs with desks that allow students to rest their feet on a bar that sways back and forth. As a hyper student growing up, I would have flourished in this chair. We need to consider innovation in every area of schooling, even the physical environment. Whether you are in a school built in the 1920s, a school that still has shag carpet, or a newly renovated school, we need to redesign how we do schooling and learning.

School Leader's Story
Empowering Students

Leader:	Winston Sakurai
School:	Hanalani Upper School
Website:	www.hanalani.org
Setting:	Suburban
Size:	350 students
Grades:	7–12
Population:	55% Asian, 24% Caucasian, 10% Pacific Islander, 4% Hispanic, 3% African American, 3% multiracial, 1% Native American
Poverty:	6% economically disadvantaged
District:	Hawaii Association of Independent Schools
Location:	Mililani, HI

Photo courtesy of Winston Sakurai

Every day is a great day for Winston Sakurai, upper school (grades 7–12) principal at Hanalani Schools in Mililani, Hawaii, because he is doing what he always wanted to be: a school principal. As a young child he saw the issues with administrator turnover, having had nine different principals from kindergarten to eighth grade. "I learned early that schools could only be great with administrators who are willing to stay and make a difference."

However, he always felt that real improvement comes because of great local leadership at the school level. When he became an administrator his first thought was to empower students to help improve their own educational journey. The school latched on to Stanford's Design Thinking process, which employs empathy and ideating to improve the lives of others. Sakurai went back to teach an applied engineering class, helping students navigate the stormy waters of collaboration and problem solving. Their big project that first year was redesigning a traditional library into a modern learning commons. Sakurai notes, "Students worked to observe patterns of

(Continued)

(Continued)

library traffic, conducted online surveys of peers and faculty, and presented a budget with furniture selections and floor layouts." The students always comment that working together was the hardest part, but they learned that you have to give and take and respect everyone's ideas. The real work happened during the summer when the students went through every library book, ripped out carpet, painted the walls, and disassembled shelving, all to create an open collaborative learning space for students at the school.

Key Chapter Takeaways

Changing the way we teach and learn has more to do with our culture and beliefs than our textbooks, architecture, or technology. To make a change in school culture it will take work to build trust, examine beliefs, and grow together as a unified community. Use the (positive) tension that results from an honest look at where you are, compared to where you want to be as a school community. These aspirations can lead to real innovation and change. Don't just pile on new ideas, decide what can be discarded, and take the necessary steps to change instructional practices across your classroom.

RELATE, INNOVATE, INVIGORATE ACTIVITIES

Relate

- Use Google Docs or Survey Monkey to conduct an anonymous survey with your students. Ask them how they would change the school structure, schedule, and physical layout, and include some open-ended questions to get ideas you may not think of at all.
- Conduct a school engagement survey; look for attitudes toward school and learning.
- Start a student forum to get feedback on your school from students.

Innovate

- Allow your staff to ask "why?" and "what if . . .?" questions. Imagine how you would design your school if you could start from scratch with your current students, staff, and community.
- Turn your mission statement into a mission question and see where your school can begin an innovation or change in practice.

- Foster student leadership by having students lead a professional development session for teachers, lead student-led parent conferences, or solicit student feedback on your school.

Invigorate

- Work with faculty, students, and staff to create a timeline of achievements for your school. Celebrate where you started, and where you've come as a learning organization.
- Have students share the positive impact teachers have on them in a faculty meeting.
- Listen to a podcast with your faculty and leadership team, and reflect on how your school has grown and needs to improve.

Team Talk: Innovate

As a School Leadership Team, assess your school's future focused leadership and learning by using Figure 4.1 and by taking the Leadership Team Self-Assessment at **www.chaselearning.org/TeamTalk**. Share your team's reflections with us.

Continue the conversation with us on Twitter at #chaselearning.

Digital Leadership, Learning, and Technology

Digital School Leaders Making a Difference for Students

"To understand their world we must be willing to immerse ourselves in that world. We must embrace the new digital reality. If we can't relate, if we don't get it, we won't be able to make schools relevant to the current and future needs of the digital generation."

—Ian Jukes

*T*his chapter will focus on the learning environments that use technology to extend and enhance both student learning and ongoing professional learning. Technology has profoundly influenced almost all aspects of our lives, including our finances, communication, health/fitness, music/media, and travel/leisure. Despite this technology-laden culture, our K–12 schools are lagging behind—and students long for relevant and authentic learning. There are examples of technology transforming learning environments, and we will share their stories and offer ways to apply their successes in other settings. Examples will be shared of school leaders, from diverse settings, on how they transformed their learning community through engaging learners and educators with the use of technology. Discussion will also include ways to improve ongoing professional learning, particularly in the area of technology integration. Digital leadership is a learned skill, and this chapter will provide concrete strategies on how to engage *your school community through the lens of technology. We will share why some schools and districts fall short with digital implementation and examine how school leaders can avoid these digital pitfalls.*

School Leader's Story
Modeling Digital Learning

Leader: Dwight Carter

School: New Albany High School

Website: http://www.napls.us/high

Setting: Suburban

Size: 1,326 students

Grades: 9–12

Population: 75% white, 10% Asian, 8% black, 4% multiracial, 3% Hispanic

Poverty: 17% economically disadvantaged

District: New Albany Plain Schools

Location: New Albany, OH

Photo courtesy of Dwight Carter

Dwight Carter is a leader of digital leadership in schools in Ohio and throughout the United States. He was recognized as one of three National Association of Secondary Schools Digital Principal Award winners in 2013, he was a Bammy Award nominee, a TEDx speaker, and his blog was ranked as one of EdTech's Top 50 Education Blogs for K–12 Education for 2016. Carter models digital leadership to his teachers by using his blog as a medium to communicate to parents, students, and his faculty and staff. He also uses Twitter to strengthen his personal learning network. Similarly, he encourages his faculty to take ownership of their own professional development by using social media and other digital tools to connect, network, and learn to grow.

Carter uses his blog to highlight a week at his school, focus on learning, or to allow a student to guest blog. We especially like how he highlights his blog into the week of school; for example, he will post on Week 32 at New Albany High School. In addition, he encourages students to serve as guest bloggers on his blog. His blog is targeted toward student learning, school events, and strategies to increase learning. A really cool feature on his blog is his page on "My Beliefs as an Education Administrator," where he explains his core beliefs as a school leader.

Carter is passionate about making sure that every student in his school is connected and that students are learning in a personalized learning culture. This culture is embedded with a focus on using technology to engage students at new levels. For example, his AP English 11 teacher, Ann Trotter, teaches a blended course, meaning part of the course is taught in a traditional format and the other half in an online format using Schoology as the learning management system. She requires students to submit assignments online, communicate in online discussions, and complete assessments via Schoology. Trotter has integrated student choice, student voice, and personalized learning into her class to engage students and to help them find success on the AP Exam. Students create a documentary film that they have written, produced, and filmed through a digital platform. They also participate in a design thinking challenge to identify a need, brainstorm a solution, and work to create a prototype to fix the problem. The digital platform in this rigorous course is a common theme in courses throughout New Albany High School.

"Digital leadership is having the courage to use today's digital resources to provide learning opportunities for students and staff, or using digital tools to engage students, staff, parents, and community members in relevant ways."

—Dwight Carter

YOU THINK YOU HAVE PROBLEMS?

For years we've been relying on the "real world" problems that textbook publishers list in their offerings. Students and teachers alike sense the disconnection between their own lives and these example problems. We suggest students stop worrying about their own (assigned) problems and start to solve somebody else's problems—real, authentic, difficult, entangled, and messy problems. Why can't students be the ones who solve our school, community, regional, or world problems?

Getting authentic problems means making connections with, and for, authentic audiences. Ideally this will allow your school to connect with a pressing, local problem that deserves attention from a large group of problem solvers in the community. Why not engage with your local township supervisors, school district maintenance supervisor, and retired engineers to have a group of science students consider a water purification solution, (re)design of a community play area, provide an HVAC solution for an aging building, or access availability for disabled community members to local attractions. These kinds of problems produce wonderful benefits for all parties involved in the problem-solving process. Students gain real-world experiences and struggles, and the community benefits from the collective wisdom and improved quality of life the solutions produce.

SwERI FRAMEWORK

Switch, Extend, Realize, Innovate. Pronounced *sw-air-eee*, this is not some sort of "text to profanity" app! These four categories create the framework to consider your digital leadership. Much like a technology model that helps us determine the level of integration (digital learning) we see in classrooms (STAR, LoTi, SAMR, etc.) the SwERI model helps us consider the effectiveness of our digital leading. Figure 5.1 shows the SwERI Framework.

SwERI provides a way for leaders to determine how their decisions are making meaningful changes for their digital learning environment. The four categories show a progression from business as usual to learning experiences that were not possible (or at least plausible in the school setting) before. It helps the future focused school leader determine if they are looking far enough down the road to make a substantive difference for their students, faculty, and community.

Switch is the first level of the framework. Switch harkens back to what Alan November discussed when he wondered if technology was *automating* a process or *informating* a process (November, 2010). This distinction came because he witnessed a lot of expensive computers entering schools to simply replace pencils. There was so much more that we knew about the writing process, but it appeared teachers were highly satisfied to let their principal know, "my students were using computers," instead of "my students were able to edit so easily that I know we will see improvements in their writing like never before." When we consider the way a learning task can change because of the technology, we are moving to the next stage.

Extend means we are taking advantage of options and capabilities that were difficult, or impossible, before the technology was used. To follow up on our writing example, we might jump ahead from the 1990s observations by Alan November and look at our own schools. Many writing exercises today are also undertaken using word processors. However, shifting to a cloud-based solution like Google Docs allows most of the functions of the word processor with some stellar additions—namely the ease of collaboration and peer editing. Now the technology allows something that was at best tedious, and at its worst maddening, for writers to share their thinking and give and receive feedback. We used a cloud-based solution to write this book, and neither of us can imagine doing it any other way.

Figure 5.1 SwERI Digital Leadership Rubric

		Description	Relate Example	Innovate Example	Invigorate Example
Sw	Switch	Technology does not change the leadership process or product, it simply switches from analog to digital.	Leader replaces e-mail with texting communication for staff and community.	Leader replaces desktop or laptop computers with notebooks, but tasks remain relatively unchanged.	Leader replaces student of the month bulletin board with social media solution to highlight role models from the student body.
E	Extend	Technology adds value or capability to the leadership process or product that was not available before.	Leader uses a blog to allow dialogue to flow in both directions, allowing professional staff and community members to respond.	Leader obtains discounted packages or portable hotspots to allow disadvantaged families to gain access at home.	Leader uses stories of schools that changed learning with technology at faculty meetings and community events.
R	Realize	Technology applied to an authentic leadership problem, process, or product, within or beyond the school system.	Leader creates digital stories to highlight teacher success and shares with professional staff and community.	Leader uses cloud-based solutions to gather informal walkthrough data and share with staff to examine collective practices at the school.	Leader gathers survey data for identified problem through a web-based form allowing students and community members to weigh in.
I	Innovate	Technology used to create a leadership process, product, or solution that would not be possible without the integration of technology.	Leader uses desktop video to gather collaborators beyond the school system for professional learning for themselves and their staff.	Leader creates mobile data collection system that allows community to generate authentic problems for students to solve.	Leader works with community partners to repurpose a physical space for entrepreneurship opportunities with community businesses.

Realize is a word we often associate with an "Aha!" moment, but the word at its root means to make something real. This is exactly what this level of the SwERI framework intends. You just read about word problems in textbooks and authentic problems in the world. When we use technology to connect with real, authentic, complex, and persistent problems, we are helping our students gain skills they will use for the rest of their lives. The Realize level also has the benefit of engaging students because we are honoring their skills to make a difference in the world right now. Too many times our K–12 students hear the message (explicitly or tacitly) that if they just hang in there, do their work, behave in school, and make it to graduation they will eventually have a chance to make a real difference. This is sad. Ironically, our agrarian society prior to World War II was a much more authentic place for school-aged children. They were a very real part of the family's ability to exist and thrive as a farm business. Math wasn't just a school lesson, it was the way eggs were boxed and gathered, prices for meat and produce were calculated, and square footage was determined for purchasing seeds. STEM was an everyday occurrence as parents and children worked together to repair engines, fix well pumps, and care for sick animals. Long before our world of specialists we were almost all generalists.

Innovation is the last stage. Given the context we just described for farm families, we seem to have gone backwards in our relevance for education. This places the importance of innovation at an all-time high. Because we now exist in a world of specialties, it's more vital than ever to collaborate, question, and create solutions together that allow us to work in ways that were not possible before. If we fail to model and teach innovation to our students, we are destined to become a nation of followers who simply implement the powerful ideas of others. Arguably the one characteristic that sets us apart as Americans is our ability to innovate, yet if we are not careful caretakers of this legacy we will lose our defining trait. High-stakes testing, and the elimination of art, music, and dance, all nip at the heels of our innovative spirit. Let's use the power of technology to nurture and grow this vital future focused skill.

Creating Your PLN

A personal learning network (PLN) has become a new standard for both lifelong personal and ongoing professional learning. Without a doubt, we have grown more from our personal learning network than any professional development we have attended. Our personal learning network has challenged our status quo, inspired us to try new things, caused us to self-reflect and examine, and spurred us on to do innovative things for our students, staff, and community. We encourage you to get engaged with a personal learning network. We would be honored to become part of that network. But we also included future focused leaders from all levels of school leadership for you to begin to learn from, connect with, and collaborate with.

One group that I have enjoyed being a part of and have grown through networking with is the Remind Advisory Board. This board of school leaders challenges me to stretch and to grow as a school leader. I also belong to several Voxer groups where I communicate regularly, work to solve problems and challenges that I face, and learn from others. This tool has inspired me to be a stronger and better school leader. Additionally, Twitter Chats have transformed my learning; by participating in Twitter Chats, I found a new outlook on school leadership. I learn new ideas, collaborate with my peers, and learn strategies to improve as a school leader. Figure 5.2 has some leaders you might consider following:

Figure 5.2   Future Focused Leaders on Twitter

Grade Level	School Leader	Twitter Handle
PreK	Nancy Alvarez	@techwnancy
PreK–5	Todd Nesloney	@TechNinjaTodd
PreK–6	Jason Borton	@Borto74
K–4	Bethany Hill	@bethhill2829
K–5	Sanée Bell	@SaneeBell
K–5	Brad Gustafson	@GustafsonBrad
6–8	Carrie Jackson	@Jackson_Carrie
6–8	Derek McCoy	@mccoyderek
6–8	John Bernia	@MrBernia
6–8	Jethro Jones	@jethrojones
6–8	Beth Houf	@BethHouf
7–12	Winston Sakurai	@winstonsakurai
9–12	Darren Ellwein	@dellwein
9–12	Dwight Carter	@Dwight_Carter
9–12	Theresa Stager	@PrincipalStager
9–12	David Geurin	@DavidGeurin
9–12	Jason Markey	@JasonMMarkey
District Administration	Neil Gupta	@drneilgupta
District Administration	Joe Sanfelippo	@Joesanfelippofc
District Administration	Hal Roberts	@HalLRoberts

(Continued)

Figure 5.2 (Continued)

Grade Level	School Leader	Twitter Handle
District Administration	A. J. Juliani	@ajjuliani
Education Leader	Daisy Dyer Duerr	@DaisyDyerDuerr
Education Leader	Justin Baeder	@eduleadership
Education Leader	Jimmy Casas	@casas_jimmy
Education Leader	Eric Sheninger	@E_Sheninger
Education Leader	Ian Jukes	@ijukes
Education Leader	Mitchel Resnick, MIT	@mres
Education Enterprise	Edutopia	@edutopia

Avoiding the Pitfalls of Digital Leadership

If we asked you to imagine a particular discipline that's using technology to transform their learning environment is there a subject that immediately comes to mind? Physical education may be an unlikely suspect, but we see a middle school program that has been transformed with the integration of one-to-one technology tools. This shift was so unexpected that the technology department underestimated the wireless access points that were needed to paint the gymnasium. One of the key shifts we've seen is the individualization of lifelong fitness through the popular workout app Sworkit. This app allows individuals or small groups of students to create a workout routine that encompasses specific exercise to target cardio, strength, flexibility, and so on and then guides the users through a workout. By offering students a framework to build within, the teachers have been able to facilitate student-led stations throughout the gym. It's amazing to see the energy and engagement students bring to the experience when they are able to create workouts, get guided instruction on screen, and receive guidance and encouragement from their teacher.

One of the great benefits of this kind of learning environment is that students can easily extend this same learning outside of the school building. I hear athletes, and non-athletes talking about the Sworkit experiences they design for themselves or their friends. Clearly, technology has helped build a lifetime fitness habit for some of our students.

FUTURE DESIGN LEARNING ENVIRONMENTS

We need to change how schools look and how we are educating our children. Why is it that retailers, medicine, businesses, churches, and health clubs are integrating technology to personalize their product, service, or message but schools are still teaching and learning in the same way as years ago? Prospective Cadillac consumers will be able to walk into a store, put on virtual reality (VR) goggles, and experience test driving, the interior, and exterior without ever sitting in an actual car. This personalization for the consumer allows for choice and the ability to experience themselves in the car of their choosing. Even the National Football League (NFL) is jumping into the world of virtual reality. In a recent article in *USA Today*, the NFL shared that Commissioner Roger Goodell participated in a virtual reality exercise to learn about empathy. The article shares that he wanted to learn more about diversity and empathy, and the virtual reality experience allowed him to do just that. The NFL also shared that teams like the Arizona Cardinals and Dallas Cowboys are using virtual reality to help players learn plays and examine their own play from a first-person perspective. (As Eagles fans, we can't believe we just included the Cowboys in this book!) Charities like the International Rescue Committee are exploring the capabilities of VR to nurture empathy and increase donorship (Sydell, 2017).

We're not saying that schools should be equipping every student with VR goggles (but hey, that would be pretty amazing), but we are saying that our work is so much more important than selling cars and the game of football. We shape and mold the future with every student, and this should cause us to rethink how we do learning. With more ubiquitous technology, augmented reality and virtual reality opportunities are becoming more affordable for schools and more convenient to take students where they have never been before. Let's take a closer look at augmented and virtual reality and get a glimpse of how it can strengthen student engagement and learning.

Virtual Reality: Taking Students Where They Have Never Been Before

Have you been to the North Pole to watch polar bears? Did you swim with sharks? We have, well not physically, but every time we use our Discovery VR cardboard goggles, we feel like we're right there in the frigid temps observing polar bears or swimming as fast as we can to get away from the great white sharks.

Do you think your students will ever get a chance to visit outer space, learn about rhinos on the move in Nepal, or trek through a rainforest to learn about ecosystems? We know few of our students will have these opportunities due to cost, time, and countless other reasons. But with virtual reality, students now can go where they have never gone before. With virtual reality, classroom doors are blown open to a world of discovery, learning, and adventure. The cost of VR is coming down every day, and now Google Cardboard makes it affordable and practical to use in a classroom. Plus, now smartphones allow users to create their VR content with ease. We would like to thank Hall Davidson, of Discovery Education, for teaching us about VR and AR at the Discovery Education Principal Summit. DENSI, the Discovery Educator Network Summer Institute, is where Dave and I learned so many amazing things for school leaders.

What we love about VR is that it allows students, regardless of their financial status, to explore and learn from experts in areas of the world that most people have never been. It gives students a 360-degree view and allows them to immerse themselves in the learning. Below are some apps that allow students and teachers to explore a world of virtual reality.

It's important that we take VR beyond students simply viewing; they need to become creators. The Greenwood Team at Brad Gustafson's school (School Leader's Story on p. 88) is transitioning to empower students to create virtual reality in art class, PE class, technology, and beyond. They use a 360 flying camera to create VRs, and they have a class set of Google Cardboard viewers to check out. Students have created several VR videos that are being used in the school to engage learners. Students should be creating VR opportunities for others similar to the students in Brad's school. We need a dose of reality, virtual reality that is to inspire and innovate for students.

To use the apps below, all you need is a smartphone and a VR cardboard. These can be purchased for a nominal fee on Amazon.

Discovery VR (http://www.discoveryvr.com): This is by far my favorite of all the VR apps. Students take field trips in remote places of the world, examine the future, learn about innovative design, and learn from the ever-popular MythBusters. The technology on this app is outstanding, and they are constantly updating the features, experiences, and viewing opportunities.

USA Today (http://www.usatoday.com/vrstories/): This free app provides readers and viewers several opportunities to explore the world through VR. Explore new areas, get an insider's perspective, and learn from various areas of the world. The site provides fresh VR videos to explore and push alerts when new VR videos are added each week. Go to the USA Today app or website and search Virtual Reality.

Google Cardboard (https://vr.google.com/cardboard/): Google Cardboard provides some VR experiences but it's also the base format for so many VR apps. This app empowers users to create their own VR experience using only their smartphone and the Google Cardboard glasses.

Google Street View (https://www.google.com/streetview/): This app allows you to see the street view of anywhere in the world. You can do this in a VR format. This provides such a rich experience for students to see the world from an entirely new perspective.

VR Flight Simulator: I always wanted to be a pilot of fast fighter jets, but my educational side also enjoys the VR Flight Simulator as it allows you to fly the plane and work to avoid the dangers of warfare. This is formatted as a game so it's important to examine age levels before using with students.

Virtual Reality Moon for Google Cardboard: This app takes you on a lunar experience like none other. It allows students to explore and experience the moon like never before.

Within - VR (Virtual Reality): This app is a curated collection of VR collections with professional filming and music that tell the stories of New York City and beyond.

Now, users can create their own VR experience with the use of panoramic cameras on smartphones, and VR cameras are becoming more affordable for educators. Soon, creating VR will be easy, accessible, and common practice. Check out this video clip for a quick tutorial on how to create your own VR experience using your smartphone: www.chaselearn ing.org/VR.

Augmented Reality

The other day, our family was eating dinner when my kids noticed our neighbors across the street wandering aimlessly around looking at the ground and parking lot. Later we found out that they were chasing Pokemons through the augmented reality app.

Augmented reality is when technology supplements, modifies, or expands our own reality. It adds a layer of media onto an actual, physical reality. It allows students to engage with technology in a manner that invades their own reality through sound and images. Augmented reality can take a student's two-dimensional drawing and make it three dimensional. It can take a child into the storyline of the book and make it seem real with images and sound. Below are easy, practical, and sustainable strategies that are being used by other school leaders throughout the world.

Aurasma App/Website (https://www.aurasma.com): Aurasma claims to bridge the digital with the physical. It turns objects, images, and just about anything into an interactive, engaging, and fun experience for students. For a quick example, download the app, allow it to access your camera, and point your camera at the backside of a one-dollar bill. You will see the dollar come to life with a video embedded in the dollar. At New Canaan High School in New Canaan, Connecticut, school leader Bill Eagan and his team use Aurasma and AR to showcase student and staff introductions and make principal trading cards that include a welcome video message for their school.

At Lecanto Middle School, in Lecanto, Florida, under the leadership of school leader Brian Lancaster and his lead teachers Maurisa Applegate and Brady Hannett, students used Aurasma to bring their yearbook to life. Students embedded videos into the yearbook that activate when a student uses the Aurasma app and points their phone camera at the image. Turn your static yearbook into an interactive book and engage readers in an entirely new way.

Other ways that school leaders can use Aurasma:

- Showcase Student Work: Aurasma is an excellent way to have students share their story, talk about how they created or solved a problem, and discuss what they learned from their work.
- Faculty Welcome: Teachers create a short video that comes to life when students point their mobile devices, with the Aurasma app, to the room number of the teacher's classroom.
- Back-to-School Night: Use Aurasma to welcome parents to Back-to-School Night and to showcase what your school is doing to engage students and support all learners.
- Art Show: Have students create a video that showcases their artwork and have the video come to life when Aurasma is used on their artwork. One school filmed time-lapsed video of the student creating the artwork, from beginning to end, and included a testimony on why the student created the work and what it means to them.
- Science Lab Safety Lessons: Use Aurasma to teach students proper behavior when working on a science lab.
- Locker Opening: From middle school to high school, opening lockers is a challenge for students. Take a pic of your locker, create a video teaching students how to open the locker, and then show teachers how to use the app.

Download the Aurasma app, open the app, and point your camera at the logo that follows.

Here are other AR apps to explore:

- Quiver (http://www.quivervision.com/apps/quiver-education/): Quiver brings coloring to life with AR and engages students in an entirely new way. Learn more about Quiver for Education at their website.
- Elements 4D (http://elements4d.daqri.com): This app and web-based program bring the elements to life through AR. Students create elements using special paper blocks that come to life when the app and camera are pointed at them. If the two elements react, students can watch as the elements become the compound created and the chemical reaction takes place right before their eyes.
- Layar (https://www.layar.com): Students and educators can enliven their work, essay, research paper, or class assignments with this fee-based interactive augmented reality tool.
- GeoGuessr (https://www.geoguessr.com): Their tagline is "Embark on a journey that will take you all over the world. From the most desolate roads in Australia to the busy, bustling streets of New York City."
- Star Walk (http://www.vitotechnology.com/star-walk.html): This is an excellent app to learn about astronomy and celestial objects. Bring the stars to students and engage with celestial objects in a whole new way.
- The Fantastic Flying Books of Mr. Morris Lessmore (http://morrislessmore.com and https://edshelf.com/tool/imag-n-o-tron/): This book is amazing and highly engaging for students. When educators download the app IMAG-N-O-TRON, they can read this book to their students and the book comes to life on their mobile device.
- AR Flashcards (http://arflashcards.com): Flashcards become interactive and highly engaging for students. They can be downloaded for free and used to teach students math, spelling, counting, and so much more.

Soar With Coding

In the future, students who know how to code will have a distinct advantage over those that don't. Coding opens up the problem-solving, analytical thinking, and programming skill set of students and allows them to explore new areas and careers. Teaching students and educators about coding can and should be highly engaging, fun, and exciting. One way that I learned to code was through flying a drone. That's right, the drone was controlled through Tynker (https://www.tynker.com), a website focused on teaching students coding. Students can have a drone flying competition by using the Tynker app to control the flight using coding. The competition can be to see who can fly the drone through an obstacle course using the coding Tynker control. Drones and coding are superb ways to engage students and to teach them coding. Parrot Drones (https://www.parrot .com/us/) are the best to use with the Tynker app. All a teacher needs is an iPad, smartphone, or laptop to have students guide and direct the drone using coding through Tynker. Plus, now students can combine VR with the drone and coding to see what the drone is filming as it flies through the air. The Tynker website is packed full with resources for teachers and parents on how to engage students with coding.

School Leader's Story
Technology Supports Student Interest

Leader: Darren Ellwein

School: Harrisburg South Middle School

Website: http://southmiddleschool .harrisburgdistrict41-2.org/

Setting: Rural

Size: 485 students

Grades: 6–8

Population: 94.4% white, 2.3% black, 1.5% Hispanic, 1.2% Asian, 0.6% multiracial

Poverty: 23.5% economically disadvantaged

District: Harrisburg School District

Location: Harrisburg, SD

Photo courtesy of Darren Ellwein

Darren Ellwein believes that investing and scheduling time for students to be creators is important when working to inspiring them to greatness. It is so important that he schedules an hour into the school day for students to create, design, and invent. He calls this the Genius Hour, and every student in the building has a Genius Hour or an EdCamp throughout the last hour of the day on Wednesdays. Student choice is key as they select what they want to focus on and learn about. Ellwein uses the national model of Genius Hour. Several students presented at conferences for teachers on their Genius Hour project, and they showcased their work to the community as a celebration.

Ellwein energized his students and his community when he gave students a chance to pursue their dreams and ambitions during Genius Hour. One seventh-grade student and his classmate did a research study on stimuli at the Great Plains Zoo as his Genius Hour project. Another student did a project on upcycling during the Genius Hour where she used items that would normally be disposed of and turned them into useful items.

According to the Genius Hour website, "Genius Hour is a movement that allows students to explore their own passions and encourages creativity in the classroom. It provides students a choice in what they learn during a set period time during school." Learn more about Genius Hour by visiting their website at http://www.geniushour.com.

Key Chapter Takeaways

Technology resources have the potential to bring relevance to learning for our digital learners—to help us speak in their language. These digital tools can also change the way leaders learn together. Technology has tremendous promise as a change force within our entrenched system of traditional schooling. Try to model the use of technology for learning by engaging with a PLN. If you already do this, make sure you let your students and staff know. If you've haven't used this strategy, start slowly, but let students and staff know you're learning in a new way. Highlight electronic collaboration for learning in faculty meetings and school events. Take an appropriate learning risk yourself and you can inspire an entire system.

RELATE, INNOVATE, INVIGORATE ACTIVITIES

Relate

- Build your own PLN and connect with local, national, and international colleagues.
- Invite community members and business partners to come in as guest speakers to launch Genius Hour activities.

- Use Aurasma to add a video introduction to each staff member's photo for Back-to-School Night. Post the photos in the lobby of your school, on their classroom door, and send home via newsletter.

Innovate

- Implement a Genius Hour event in your school. Consider making it part of your master schedule.
- Host Hour of Code or Genius Hour in your school to promote digital learning.
- Use Google Cardboard to create a virtual reality video to showcase a lesson or activity to your community.

Invigorate

- Use the learning management system of your district to create a course for faculty that focuses on instructional practices for technology use.
- Have a class join a Discovery Learning virtual reality field trip.
- Join our Remind Class to get regular encouragement to innovate. Join the class at remind.com/join/chaselrng.

Team Talk: Innovate Together

As a school leadership team, assess your leadership team's digital leadership skill set using the SwERI model. Identify areas of strength, deltas (areas needing change), and growth areas. Go to **www.chaselearning .org/SwERI** and take the interactive SwERI assessment with your leadership team.

Continue the conversation with us on Twitter at #chaselearning.

Nurturing Creativity

Strategies for Leaders to Inspire Creativity in Their Teachers, Students, and Parents

"You need courage to be creative. Just as soon as you have a new idea, you are a minority of one. And being a minority of one is uncomfortable—it takes courage!"

—E. Paul Torrance

"I think if you do something and it turns out pretty good, then you should go do something else wonderful, not dwell on it for too long. Just figure out what's next."

—Steve Jobs

Many people believe creativity is something you're born with—or you lack. Using the growth vs. fixed mindset work of Dr. Carol Dweck and the creativity research of E. Paul Torrance, we will offer ways to nurture and grow the creativity of the school leader and their organization. Creativity can be learned, and this chapter will offer practical exercises and approaches to draw out the most creative solutions to problems facing your organization. This chapter is an action chapter; there will be exercises that school leaders can engage in immediately to stretch their creative thinking, inspire creativity within their school community, and instill a spirit of creativity within their school.

School Leader's Story
Creating Space for Creativity

Leader: Brad Gustafson

School: Greenwood Elementary School

Website: http://www.wayzata.k12.mn.us/Domain/10

Hashtag: #GWgreats

Setting: Suburban

Size: 730+ students

Grades: K–5

Population: 83% white, 13% Asian, 3% Hispanic, 1% African American

Poverty: 5% economically disadvantaged

District: Wayzata Public Schools

Location: Plymouth, MN

Photo courtesy of Brad Gustafson

When it comes to championing creativity, Brad Gustafson believes that nobody does it better than students themselves. That's why the Greenwood Elementary team strives to amplify student voice while shifting additional ownership of the learning to kids.

Gustafson is in his seventh year as principal at Greenwood Elementary, and in that time he's seen his staff implement numerous practices designed to nurture creativity. He prefers to support student creativity through modeling, not mandates.

- Student of the Month, celebrating Creativity, Innovation, and Effort (*not* just academic achievement)
- Spark Plug Award for staff (what are we celebrating and looking for?)
- Student Podcasting (I always say, "It's amazing what kids can create when we love them, believe in them, and get out of their way!")
- Mobile Makerspace Fleet (staff and student input . . . high-tech, low-tech, and no-tech tools)
- Multiple Lego Walls (access and intentionality)
- Shining the light on student creativity using live-streaming, social media, blogging, as well as traditional means.
- "Grizzly Gallery," celebrating the creative genius in every child (explicitly name it to show you value it)
- Passport to Passion night (specialist conferences with parents)
- Little things like sitting in on art classes and creating alongside kids.

THE FOURTH REVOLUTION

According to the *Future of Jobs Report: Employment, Skills and Workforce Strategy for the Fourth Industrial Revolution* (World Economic Forum, 2016), creativity is not just a nice idea for our students, but a sought-after commodity. They state, "Creativity will be one of the top three required skills by the year 2020. Workers will need to seek out novel solutions, apply knowledge in different ways, and consider options for problems that have never before existed." We begin our chapter on nurturing creativity with yet another authentic, compelling reason to grow this vital skill in our students and staff.

Efficient Is No Longer Sufficient

Let's consider the context that either nurtures or squelches creativity. Many of the external pressures related to K–12 school systems in the past 20 years stem from a legislative desire to adopt a more "business-minded" approach. While we can all learn from multiple disciplines, many business models are underpinned by the concept of efficiency. Often this efficiency thinking fights against investing the time for creativity and risk taking. Ironically, some of the most successful business ventures of all time thrive on innovation and creativity (e.g., Apple, Google, Amazon.com).

If we dig deeper we find efficiency is not the limiting issue, but complacency is. To say this another way, the arch nemesis of creativity and innovation is status quo. If you never question the processes and methods you're engaging in you are unlikely to stumble into meaningful innovation or creative solutions. Failure to question the status quo (due to time constraints, deadlines, or complacency) results in business as usual. If we never stop to question, the potential outcome is that our schools become almost entirely irrelevant for 21st-century digital learners and their leaders. Let's look at two big ideas to turn the tide toward innovation and creativity: elegant questions and staying a little longer.

Elegant Questions

Changing the status quo begins with beautiful questions. e. e. Cummings wrote, "Always the beautiful answer / Who asks the more beautiful question." Author Warren Berger highlights the same quote and believes questioning is the heart of creating breakthrough ideas (Berger, 2014). Sadly, our own school experiences as students are likely to mirror what we see in most classrooms today—an emphasis on answers instead of questions. Too often the explicit, or implicit, message to students is that correct answers matter most, and mistakes are a sign of intellectual weakness.

Some talented students learn to "play school" and discover they can feign attention, ask a few low-level recall questions, and often get the teacher to deliver the answer for them.

This is not the kind of questioning we seek. Questions that lead to creative solutions and innovate practices rely on a balance that allows a big question that's also attainable. A school struggling to get parent involvement might ask, "Why do we expect parents to come to our door? Could we get better engagement and participation in conferences if we left the schoolhouse and went into the neighborhood?" This question could lead to teachers and administrators gathering with parents in community centers, supermarket cafes, or other local businesses.

The leader who embraces questioning is also giving away power. As a school leader you may counsel a teacher who reacts sharply when a student asks, "Why do we need to know this?" Perhaps your immediate response leans toward stressing relevance and encouraging staff members to make connections between their core learning goals and students' lives. Do you keep the same open mind when a teacher interrupts a faculty meeting with a question like, "Why are we still doing referrals this way?" Giving away power can create the kind of environment where every person is empowered to question, reflect, and of course, suggest solutions. Elegant questioning is not the same as a complaining session.

Edward de Bono, The Right Question Institute, Warren Berger, and others have suggested a pattern of questioning that leads to innovation and creativity (Berger, 2014; de Bono, 1999). It involves three specific types of questions in a suggested order. They advocate beginning with "Why?" questions, followed by "What if . . . ?" questions. These two types should be engaged until multiple possibilities emerge. Don't move too quickly or you might miss your best solution (as you'll learn in the next section). After sufficient time here your team will move to the "How?" questions as the implementation of your solution/innovation works out. The first two types of questions require more of a divergent thinking approach, and the last type warrants a more practical, rubber-meets-the-road kind of thinking.

Staying a Little Longer

The creative photographer or painter often views exactly the same scene as we do—sometimes our most ordinary surroundings—yet manages to create something powerful, poignant, and elegant. One way they accomplish this result is by staying a little longer. This could mean actually staying at a physical location for a longer period, rereading a portion of text over and over, or more likely it means we intentionally return to an idea or situation purposefully in our thinking. It might be "inefficient" to not immediately act, but if we can hold out and resist the immediate response/action the better solution will emerge. We can improve our own creativity by intentionally resisting the pressure for an immediate solution. Force yourself to formulate multiple solutions for the problem/challenge, and use a team of people to help create possible solutions.

Dwelling in a space (physically or mentally) helps us see something that is passed over with a quick glance or short visit. Okay, time for another practical application we promised. This one is called "Stop, Unprop, and Troll." It's a sure-fire way to extinguish complacency.

- *Stop* what you're doing and walk to your office.
- *Unprop* and close the door so no one interrupts you.
- *Troll* for new perspectives/ideas on a goal or task you're working on.
- *Ponder* a concern/problem/process that you'd like to change or improve. (Consider using the "Why?" and "What if . . . ?" questions mentioned above.)
- *Choose* some way to get your thinking out that works for you. This might mean a running journal of ideas you create with Google Docs, a physical journal, voice memos you dictate to your phone, a graphic organizer, a blog that you keep for this purpose and never make public, or any other method you like. Just be sure to record your thinking so you can return to this "document" next time you can Stop, Unprop, and Troll. (Once a direction emerges, move to "How?" questions.)

Engaging in a time for reflection is the heart of this activity, and creativity experts from multiple disciplines almost always acknowledge an incubation period as an important part of the creative process. Allowing the brain to churn on an idea in the conscience activity of Stop, Unprop, and Troll will also spur the brain toward the unconscious processing that often births (incubates) an idea. When solutions begin to emerge don't settle on the first idea that comes to mind. Push yourself to stay a little longer in the solutions phase as well, and have two or three (or 20) ideas to compare.

Improvise

This word strikes fear in the heart of many, especially the idea of improvised, extemporaneous public speaking. Others hear "improvise" and know it's a foundational element in jazz music, but they wonder how it connects with school leadership. We believe there are lessons to learn about improvisation that will help school leaders innovate and move their learning organizations forward. Two key areas to consider relate to embracing mistakes and working within limited options.

Embrace Mistakes

Educational researchers like Carol Dweck, Jo Boaler, Sir Ken Robinson, and others have helped us see the power of mistakes while learning (Boaler, 2016; Dweck, 2016; Robinson, 2011). As educational leaders we can reap benefits from mistakes and failures. The stakes are high for us in the arena of public opinion that seems to grow more and more intense for K–12 schools. However, the fear of mistakes can paralyze our change efforts and ensure we will never rise above the status quo. If we want to grow there will be growing pains, and some of those pains will be directly related to errors, mistakes, and failures.

Jazz students often avoid improvisation because they fear playing a wrong note. Don't forget these scared performers are most likely correct: If they improvise a solo they will probably make a mistake—or several mistakes—in a very short period of time. Great artists like Charlie Parker, Miles Davis, and Thelonious Monk took notes that were considered "mistakes" and created entirely new genres. Some of our most important advances in society were aided by mistakes along the way. Consider penicillin, the incandescent light bulb, sticky notes, and many others.

One technique that helps early improvisers is to use only one note to begin improvising. Does this sound too limiting? We'll talk more about that in a minute, but for now consider what one note can do for you. Don't forget that one musical note, like one word in a conversation, can convey many moods by the way it's played. Is the note loud or soft? Does it last a long time or happen very quickly then disappear? Does it start with a little slide or begin exactly on pitch? Is the sound mellow and relaxed or intense and focused? Does it repeat in a regular pattern, or happen sporadically?

Work With Limited Options

One aspect that scares new improvisers is the thought of boundless options. In the case of a writing task this same phenomenon is referred to as black-page syndrome. It's important to remember that creating "something out of nothing" is not really what we human beings do. Our best efforts toward creativity and innovation always involve working, or more accurately reworking, the finite resources we have at our disposal. The trick is finding new ways to interconnect materials and ideas to form a new, synthesized, and hopefully elegant solution that was not in place. Let's look at the musician who's learning to improvise for some lessons we can apply to school leadership.

If I asked you to sit at a piano and "make something up" that's completely original would you be able to do it? Does the idea completely paralyze you? Does a seasoned professional player have any advantage in this situation? Have you ever tried it yourself? Do you feel similar pressure as you look across your learning organization and wonder if you can create something completely new and different that is more effective for our changing landscape? First I want to let you know that I have high confidence that anyone reading this paragraph could be guided to create something to satisfy the challenge of the first sentence. The first thing to consider is the constraints you probably placed on the task yourself. Did you think about trying to create a classical piano piece? A Billboard Hit that's a piano ballad? Neither example, or any other genre, was in the task itself. Maybe you just panicked because you envisioned those 88 keys and had no idea which ones you need to strike, in which order, to "make music." Time for another hands-on creativity exercise—the piano challenge. Use these steps:

- Get to a piano or electronic keyboard. If you don't have access at home, school, or church, you could visit a music store.
- Try pressing keys, using one or both hands, to create a song.
- Impose a limited time on your song like 30, 45, or 60 seconds.
- Try again with the form of a story we teach emerging writers, keeping "beginning, middle, end" in mind.
- Take several attempts; don't stop with your first "ideas."
- Pause and reflect. Have you created music? Is it worth listening to?

If you haven't tried the exercise above, *do not read* this paragraph. Skip ahead until you can try the task at a piano or keyboard, and bring your book with you. I'm going to give you two, simple limitations that will probably improve your song significantly—especially if you do not play any musical instrument. The first is to only strike the black keys. These keys actually comprise a specific relationship of pitches that allows for a "no wrong note" feeling as you play. Awkward "sour notes" that may have plagued your first attempts will disappear. The second is to think of a simple sentence and use the syllables of the words to create a rhythm for your hands/notes. Something like, "Chicago deep dish pizza is a tasty meal." Use the natural ebb and flow of speech to guide you; avoid a monotone reading. Now, try the song challenge again. How did your creation change?

Can you find parallel applications to your own school leadership? Does the task of creating a school for the future paralyze you? We all have stakeholders watching this process. Could you imagine how much harder the piano challenge would be with an audience on hand? I hope you can see that limited time, insufficient funding, and inadequate facilities certainly have an impact on our work, but they should never be ultimate determiners for our creative problem solving. Embrace your resources and find ways to move toward the new reality you have in mind for your organization. Peter Senge (2006) values the cognitive dissonance between where your organization is and where you want it to be as a key force for change. Use this energy in your work.

GROWING CREATIVITY

One way to immediately grow the creativity in your organization is to increase opportunities for collaborative problem solving. This requires the leader to share power and control, but the benefits are substantial. Consider a few examples to demonstrate the power of collaboration for creativity. If I ask you to name a creative movie producer you might suggest Steven Spielberg, George Lucas, Walt Disney, Martin Scorsese, Spike Lee, or other famous leaders. Famous leaders who have produced billions of dollars of revenue from their films, but how many people helped them accomplish the creative work? You might be surprised by the number of people needed to take a full-length feature film from concept to screenplay, production, distribution, marketing, and release. Of course, this varies greatly with the budget of the project, but we've all seen name after name roll in the closing credits. Stephen Follows analyzed the 50 highest-grossing films of the past 20 years on the IMDb website. His work provides a few examples of personnel involved with film making: *Avatar*, 2,984; *Iron Man 3*, 3,310. Follows states, "On average the top films of the past two decades have each had 3.5 writers, 7 producers, 55 people in the art department, 32 in sound, 55 in camera/electrical and 156 in visual effects" (Follows, 2014).

Our schools will not have Hollywood budgets, so what about a smaller, more personal creative endeavor: creating a hit song. Many people think the artist credited with the song is the sole creative force behind it, yet this misconception of "solo, creative individual" is the exception. Many solo artists don't even create the songs they perform. Instead our most well-known songs are usually crafted by a team of three to eight writers. They may specialize (lyrics, melodies, programming, etc.) but the songs we know best are often born from a collaborative process.

What's the lesson? No matter how creative you are don't overlook the boost you can achieve by practicing creativity with a team. This is also really good news if you feel like you're not very creative! Surround your-self with a creative team and contribute your specialty/strength for the overall success of the endeavor.

Additional Practice Activities

Be Prolific: How many ways can you draw something or come up with options? As you work don't stop the brainstorming or criticize solutions. Gather first and evaluate later. Don't select a solution too early—come up with at least seven solutions before selecting one.

Take Another Perspective: Use the example of a RAFT (Role, Audience, Format, Topic) activity for your leadership decisions and solutions. For example, write a funding proposal/solution to your superintendent as a student, parent, teacher, and principal.

Create Space: Dedicate a space in your school for everyone to add ideas. This might be a whiteboard in the hallway, a mind map in the faculty room, or a virtual space online for students, teachers, and parents. You can center the ideas on a topic of growth/concern, or keep it wide open and see what emerges.

Activate Your Brain: One of the most amazing activities we've seen to break out of your comfort zone in a low-risk way uses a line drawing/sketch. Take the image and place it upside-down in front of you. On a blank piece of paper, use your nonwriting hand to copy the drawing. After completing your copy turn the original and put your copy beside it. Does it appear stronger than you ever imag-ined? Consider how you "thought differently" when you were drawing.

Test Creativity: You know by now that we are not fans of high-stakes testing, so this is not one more assessment piled on for your students. E. Paul Torrance did foundational research in the field of creativity at the University of Georgia (Torrance, 1995). One outcome of his work is the Torrance Test of Creative Thinking (TTCT). This is unlike any traditional test you've seen, and portions of his measures are available online. By addressing figural creativity (drawing and interpreting shapes and lines) and aspects of creativity like being prolific, Torrance creates a way for the creative individual to demonstrate capabilities that are not present in traditional standardized measures.

The TTCT might be a screening tool for giftedness, or simply a way to show students and staff that creativity is not easily measured with traditional instruments.

School Leader's Story
Creative Solutions for Authentic Problems

Leader: Glenn Robbins

School: Northfield Community Middle School

Website: http://northfield.groupfusion.net/

Setting: Suburban

Size: 889 students

Grades: 5–8

Population: 84% white, 8% Hispanic, 5% Asian, 3% black

Poverty: 22.6% economically disadvantaged (2014 data)

District: Northfield Community School

Location: Northfield, NJ

Photo courtesy of Glenn Robbins

Anyone who walks through Northfield Community School can feel the creativity flowing through the students, teachers, and principals. Whether it is hallways turned into Idea Street, students creating prosthetic limbs, or students working in the Makerspace, this creativity has taken Glenn Robbins and his teachers to the White House. His school has become a leader in Makerspaces and designing creative learning spaces for students.

Robbins shares, "Our school embraces many 'original' practices, such as: daily ungraded student led EdCamp periods, an ungraded Digital Shop focused on empathic human centered design thinking, personalized learning for students through a learning management system (LMS), and Idea Streets (hallways) that encourage learning anywhere, at any time. Idea Streets are nontraditional hallways that replaced bulletin boards with white boards. They allow anyone to ride stationary bike desks, work at surfboard bars, watch turtles swim in a revamped trophy case, use an 80-inch by 80-inch Lego board, or sit in small groups at the high top tables and/or Hokki stools. We even allow students to select the furniture they would like in our school. With a building that is fully Wi-Fi, why should learning always be limited to the four walls of a traditional classroom led by a teacher? Fortunately, we have an outstanding staff that have bought into our creative/maker culture and climate that thrives on autonomy to better the lives of the whole student to be Life Ready."

Recently, Robbin's students shipped their creations to change the lives of students overseas. His students, using the 3D printer and other school resources, created prosthetic limbs for children who are missing arms. The teacher, Kevin Jarrett, used the Enable Community Foundation for design to connect his students with prostheses recipients from around the world. Students customize the prosthetic to the child's dimensions and then work collaboratively to design, produce, and ship these gifts of new life to the recipients.

Teachers often discuss the need to engage at-risk students; nonetheless, they continue to repeat what they have always done. As school leaders, Robbins believes that we need to allow staff and students to design, iterate, and act, tens to hundreds of times, in pursuit of reaching their goals to better the lives of others. His school uses faculty meetings as meaningful professional development, makerspace challenges, reflection time, and 20% time, instead of lecturing to staff. They use extra substitutes to allow teachers to observe fellow staff during the day, and stress that lessons are to be empowering, instead of reading from PowerPoints. As leaders, Robbins shared that we must end the silos at middle and secondary education that continue to remove "wonder, curiosity, and originality" out of our students and staff. Robbins shared how it's important for leaders to believe in hiring and developing leaders. He shares, "At our school, we stress the importance of growth mindsets, and bringing out the best in others."

The Northfield staff focuses on the power of vocabulary and removed regularly misused buzzwords: 21st century, Fail, STEM, STEAM, Digital Citizenship, Innovation Is Tech. These words are immersed in every course, and not just specialized pockets of excellence within the building. Under Robbin's leadership, he makes it a priority to communicate with the teachers' union president on a daily basis to work together as one for the betterment of the building, instead of being separate teams. He also works constantly with the director of curriculum and instruction, as well as the director of informational technology, to ensure that the vision moves forward as a creative team.

Creative leadership is about being willing to ask, "what if, how might we, and/or yes and," when staff and students present them with ideas. We need to stifle the mentalities of CYBOs (Chief Yeah But Officers) in our buildings and provide them with the servant leadership that they desire. Anything is possible, if you're willing to work hard for it, and ask "Why not our school?"

Key Chapter Takeaways

You can be more creative than you are right now. Creativity is a mindset, and proper questioning can help all of us increase our creative capacity and creative output. Creating space to reflect, allowing incubation time when considering a problem/decision, or just resisting the urge to get a "quick solution" can support you, and your team, to achieve stronger, more creative solutions to the problems you encounter. Putting yourself in a new, novel, even uncomfortable position can help you practice improvisation. If you are a musician, dancer, or visual artist, try to approach your creative work in a fresh way. If you don't engage in creative arts, give it a try. Approaching learning in a novel way can be very helpful, especially for adult learners. Most importantly, nurture the mindset that reminds us we can all be creative. It's based on some genetic predisposition, or innate ability—it's also something we can build capacity for both individually and as a learning organization.

RELATE, INNOVATE, INVIGORATE ACTIVITIES

Relate

- Place a marker board in a public space and collect ideas. Nurture creativity with a prompt or problem, or allow authentic items to emerge.
- Share your creative work with students and staff in small groups and ask students to do the same. You'll be amazed at the number of students with their own portfolio of work.
- Try some of the creativity exercises in the chapter with a colleague; share your results with others. Reflect on the learning for leaders.

Innovate

- Design a place for creativity. Create a Makerspace or Breakerspace in your school.
- Design a new logo for your school or new initiative/focus for the year.
- Work with students to code an app for your school.

Invigorate

- Sit in an art or music class and actually join the students as they create art and music. Produce, perform, and collaborate.
- Make one of your display cases a mini gallery and feature a student or staff artist. Celebrate their work and encourage the school to value artistry and creativity.
- Enter your students in Google Doodle, or hold a similar contest at your school for your website, yearbook, or banner.

Team Talk

Team Talk Stories is a conversation space for school leadership teams to share their stories from experiences with the Team Talk activities at the end of each chapter.

To help build your creative school/classroom we encourage your leadership team to create 10 or 20 (maximum) questions that can be rated from 1 to 4. Create your Creative School Survey and gather responses from your staff, and have your students respond to the same questions—and then examine the two sets of results as a leadership team. Where do you find alignment? Where are the gaps in perception? Summarize your findings in a short video and share it at the Team Talk site. Find sample questions at **www.chaselearning.org/TeamTalk**.

Continue the conversation with us on Twitter at #chaselearning.

Inspiring Others to Greatness

Principals Inspiring Teachers, Students, and Parents for Amazing Things

"Whatever one's style, every leader, to be effective, must have and work on improving his or her moral purpose. Moral purpose is about both ends and means."

—Michael Fullan

"Innovation distinguishes between a leader and a follower."

—Steve Jobs

*T*he way our culture looks at school leaders has changed dramatically in recent decades. Fewer and fewer students are entering the field of education, and those that step into school leadership roles are often overwhelmed by opposition they face locally, regionally, and nationally. This reality has eroded the higher call of educating our children, and invigorating that moral purpose again has benefits at all levels of the school! The chapter will include stories and strategies to re-engage leaders, teachers, parents, and the community to embrace the work at hand. These real-life examples of school leaders will be replicable for any school leader to do in their own school and community. Never before has education been so important for our children's lifelong success, or our nation's position in the world economy.

School Leader's Story
Getting All Voices Heard

Leader: Bethany Hill

School: Central Elementary School

Website: http://www.cabotschools.org/schools/central-elementary

Setting: Rural

Size: 440 students

Grades: K–4

Population: 98% white, 2% other

Poverty: 54% economically disadvantaged

District: Cabot Public Schools

Location: Cabot, AR

Photo courtesy of Bethany Hill

If you call Bethany Hill a principal, she will affectionately share that her teachers and students know her as a lead learner of Central Elementary School. This is because she strives to keep learning at the heart of everything she does. She is a passionate leader who is committed to building caring relationships, engaging students, and inspiring everyone in her school community to greatness. She has created a school blog where she says, "Our school blog is for kids, teachers, staff, families, and community members who would like to contribute. We want to model blogging for our kids while promoting digital citizenship for them." The blog includes posts from teachers, parents, a police officer, and her rocking awesome elementary school students. One post from a first grader talked about a beaver becoming a platypus. The blog inspires others to greatness by giving them a platform to the world, a venue to showcase their best work, and an opportunity to collaborate with members of the school.

Hill shares a little about her school: "Central is an amazing place where staff place kids first always. Our mantra is 'Helping Kids Discover Their Genius,' and we do this by tapping into the interests and passions of our children. This cannot be accomplished without doing the same for adult learners. Our teachers and staff need a voice and to be empowered through their service. One way we have encouraged teacher and student voice is through our Central School Family Blog. This is a place where kids, staff, families, and the community can share ideas and reflections. Our goal is to model digital citizenship and the power of an audience. Kids who have contributed are so proud of the fact that their story is shared for all who choose to read it. Two teachers who contributed had never written a blog post before publishing to our school blog, and they serve as a model for our kids and the rest of the staff. We have only just begun our efforts to promote voice within our school family, but we are well on our way to becoming stronger each day! My dream for our school blog is for more contributors to step forward and take a risk by sharing their thoughts with the world. We are better together, and we can achieve greatness by having our voices heard."

MAKING A LASTING DIFFERENCE

We believe firmly that one of the greatest and most powerful callings of every school leader is to make a lasting difference in the lives of others and to empower others to do the same. This reminds me of a visit I took to the Statue of Liberty. While at the national landmark, I read this quote: "Give me your tired, your poor, your huddled masses yearning to breathe free, the wretched refuse of your teeming shore. Send these, the homeless, tempest-tost (sic) to me, I lift my lamp beside the golden door!" (Lazarus, 1883).

The sonnet by Emma Lazarus inspired me as a school leader because it challenged me to remember the needs of every child regardless of the color of their skin, national and ethnic origin, sexual orientation, financial level, learning ability, religion, gender, or social status. As school leaders, we are responsible for the success of every student that walks through our schoolhouse doors. The students entering our schools right now, and future students, are different—no vastly different, than when we were in school. Our nation's and our school's demographics have shifted dramatically through the years, and this requires us as school leaders to shift and change. School leaders need to be aware of these demographics, understand how to reach each student, and recommit to the high calling to make a difference in the life of every student.

Teachers need to embrace the dynamic shift in our schools and create relevant environments for students. The school leader sets the tone for this new community by embracing change and moving forward with actions that welcome all students and value the contributions each person has to offer. The shift in technology has taken many leaders by surprise, not because they didn't see it coming, but because they failed to see its relevance. Too many schools spent hours fighting the cell phone battle instead of investing the time needed to understand what future focused learning might look like in their school.

Technology is only one aspect of schooling that has changed since we sat in the classroom ourselves. There are equally broad changes in the demographics of our school (ethnicity, gender identification, and families living in poverty), the continuing reliance on high-stakes testing for school success (ranking of school, school report cards, etc.), school choice (private, magnet, charter, online), students with a parent in prison, and local/national media that present the worst we have to offer in U.S. schools in an endless 24/7 news cycle.

Making a lasting difference is hard work and requires attention to hiring, persistence, collaboration, and a tireless commitment. This can be accomplished by school leaders of all personality types; you don't need to be the cheerleading pom principal or the loud and charismatic school leader to inspire others to greatness. The calm and steady school leader can be just as effective as the abstract visionary thinker who is constantly dreaming up ways to impact their school. It's not a personality type but a leadership style—one that puts others first, empowers others, focuses on the best in people, celebrates successes, embraces failure, promotes creativity, establishes routines, trusts their team, communicates often, and makes every decision based on what is best for students. Future focused school leaders understand that our students and schools are in dire need of leaders who truly believe our best days are still ahead of us.

The overwhelming mandates from the state and federal government, standardized assessments, and the litigious culture can begin to weigh heavily on school leaders. Comply with mandates but invest in lives; don't let mandates paralyze you from making a real difference in the lives of students. When school leaders are focused on making a lasting difference, an entire school culture is changed and lifted. Educators within the school begin to see their mission as more than achieving high scores on standardized assessments; they become invested in making a difference in the lives of their students. School leaders need to set the tone that students and educators are more important than test scores, that true learning is embedded with rich and trusting relationships, and that this work can be invigorating and fun again.

> *"Comply with mandates but invest in lives; don't let mandates paralyze you from making a real difference in the lives of students."*

We all need to return to the reason we became an educator: "To make a difference in the lives of students."

CULTURE CHANGES IN EDUCATION

One of the first shifts in the world of education is the public perception of the field itself, and the resulting incentive to bring new teachers into our schools. An *Education Week* report pointed to steep enrollment declines in teacher preparation programs at the college level, saying "nationwide, enrollments in university teacher-preparation programs have fallen by about 10 percent from 2004 to 2012, according to federal estimates from the U.S. Department of Education's postsecondary data collection" (Sawchuk, 2014). The same report noted declines in California's enrollment based on a report from their credentialing organization. According to the report, the Golden State lost some 22,000 teacher-prep enrollments, or 53%, between 2008–2009 and 2012–2013. New York and Texas also saw steep declines. California, New York, and Texas are among the largest producers of teachers in all 50 states.

It's not just teacher preparation programs that are shifting. If you think students in poverty is something that doesn't apply to you, consider the fact that in early 2015 we reached a tipping point when 51% of all students in United States public schools came from homes that met the federal standards for poverty (Jensen, 2016). According to Jensen's research, this trend increased from 2005 when 16% of students lived in households of poverty to 22% by 2010—a 37.5% increase. By 2011 one in four school-age children (25%) lived in a family below the poverty line (Federal Interagency Forum on Child and Family Statistics, 2011).

The demographic landscape and needs of our students have changed dramatically over the years. School leaders need to embrace the change and celebrate the differences that make us a melting pot school system. True future focused school leaders understand these changes, identify relevant strategies to support these changes, and celebrate the diversity that comes from our constantly changing school culture. As you read through the next section, ask yourself which strategies might immediately help you as a school leader.

Understand the Changing Culture

In this section, we will discuss the various changes that are taking place in our schools and share strategies for school leaders to immediately implement in their schools. The data below are shared from the National Center for Educational Statistics (2014a, 2014b, 2016).

Race/Ethnicity

The Hispanic student population is the fastest-growing race in our nation's schools. This comes with an increasing language barrier that schools need to support and overcome. Data show that the white and black student populations are decreasing, with the Hispanic, Asian, Pacific Islander, and multiracial categories growing in the coming years. Here are some strategies to support these racial groups:

- Equal Opportunity: It's key to make sure all students are given the same opportunities for success. Take a look at your Honors, AP, and higher-level courses; do these courses reflect the racial makeup of your school? When you design school communications, include all races in the pictures and videos to reflect the population of the whole school.

- Role Models: Students see role models like them. The best way is to have a staff member that represents their race but also be sure to select assembly speakers, texts, and materials that reflect the diversity of your school.
- Translate: Have print communications translated into the languages that are represented in your schools. Use your district's world language teachers and students, or a translation service. Google Translate is a fairly reliable, safe, and free resource.
- ESL: It's important that schools have strong English as second language programs in their schools to support students who need this most important resource.

Religion

School leaders need to nurture a school environment where students of various religions are respected and accepted by students and educators. Whether your community is primarily Muslim, Christian, Jewish, Mormon, Jehovah Witness, atheist, agnostic, or any other religion, it's important that school leaders protect the religious expression of every student.

- Know Your Religious Rights: It's important for school leaders to be aware of the various religious rights that students and educators are afforded. This will go a long way in protecting you and your school. Go to www.chaselearning.org/resources for websites to learn more about religious rights.
- Honor the First Amendment: Students have a right to express their religion while at school; they don't shed their religious rights at the schoolhouse door. Students may infuse faith into class projects, speeches, artwork, and other areas that allow for the individual expression of students. Schools cannot shudder at the sight of religion brought forth by students; instead, they need to know the rights of students and staff members.
- Honor Religion: Far too often, school leaders whitewash their school of any form of religion, such as religious music at concerts, holiday celebrations, and more.
- Include Clergy: Clergy are a key member of the community to include in committees, meetings, and school activities. They often have the pulse to the community and can be a rich resource for school leaders.

Sexual Orientation

Sexual orientation and transgenderism are sensitive topics throughout our country and especially for school leaders. It's important to remember that these students are all of our students, no matter what! We have a responsibility to protect *all* students—this includes LGBTQ+ and transgender students. School leaders need to support every student regardless of their sexual orientation or transgender status.

- Start Talking: Don't ignore this group of students; it's key that your community begin to discuss sexual orientation and transgender students. If not already done, work with your district leadership to write school policy on this most important issue.
- Protect: Without a doubt, these students are bullied more than any other demographic group; as a result, school leaders must create a safe, bullying-free, and accepting school culture. Meet with your GSA group and reassure them that you are committed to protecting them. You will not stand for any harassment, ridicule, or discrimination.
- Learning: Work to educate students, teachers, parents, and the community on the various needs of these students. Talk about pronoun usage, privacy, lavatory usage, dress, and so much more.
- NASSP has issued an excellent resource for school leaders on transgender students. Check it out at www.chaselearning.org/resources.

Transient

If you have been a school leader for a year or more, you understand how transiency can negatively impact a child's education. When students are moving multiple times a year, schools are challenged to grow their learning during a short period of time when we can care for them.

- Hand Off: School leaders should work to make sure that students who leave your school land on their feet. This can be done by contacting the receiving school and sharing learning needs, important issues, and interventions that you provided.
- Send-Off Gift: Provide the student with a token or gift from your school. This helps them to remember your school and the various relationships they established. Gifts can be notes of encouragement from teachers, a yearbook, a T-shirt, or a handwritten note from the school leader. These small tokens can go a long way in inspiring the student to stay focused in their new school.
- Protect Instruction: For students that you know will be leaving your school shortly, protect instructional time and give them the

essential components to be successful at the next level. Many times, these skills are resilience, grit, hard work, communication, collaboration, and leadership.

Poverty

More and more students are coming to school with less—less money, less food, and less resources to be successful in school. This poses serious challenges for schools but also amazing opportunities to help these students rise above poverty and soar into post-secondary education. School leaders have a moral responsibility to close the achievement gap with these students and provide the tools to be successful in the future. Below are some strategies that school leaders can immediately execute to support these students

- Backpack Programs: Like James Orichosky, principal of Bald Eagle Area Elementary School, demonstrates in Chapter 9, schools can partner with businesses and community organizations to send children home with food, resources, and supplies for school.
- A Supporting Adult: These students need to have a strong rapport and relationship with an adult in the school—an adult that cares for them, invests in them, and believes in their success. They need to know someone in the school believes in them, cares for them, and will support them.
- Teaching: Teach students the norms of the school, the language and syntax of adults and learning, and the expectations of learning.
- Established Interventions: More often than not, students from poverty are behind in their learning. School leaders need to plan and establish individualized interventions that can serve as a safety net to help these students reach their potential and to close the achievement gap.
- Relationships, Relationships, Relationships: It cannot be said enough, educators need to build positive, caring, and supportive relationships with the students and their parents. This can be accomplished by visiting the home, providing food and gifts during the holidays, providing jackets during the winter, and helping the parents find success. This success may be helping them enroll in a GED class or a community college, allowing them to access the school's technology, and having your teachers run parent lessons on job interviewing strategies, child care, or financial planning.

Gender

Title IX has highlighted the need to provide equal opportunities in athletics. But this equality needs to flow into all areas of the academic world. Making sure that you are challenging and encouraging girls to take high-level math and science courses and boys in English and the arts is key. School leaders need to introduce STEAM (Science, Technology, Engineering, Arts, and Math) with both genders in mind.

- Expectations: From elementary school until graduation, school leaders should be providing opportunities that shatter that status quo in regard to gender. On a personal note, we are both fathers to sons and daughters and we are passionate about making sure our girls are given the same opportunities and experiences that our boys are given.
- Role Model: It's important that our girls see females in leadership in all areas and facets of the workplace. Help us to shatter the glass ceiling and encourage our girls to do great things in their school, community, and world. Bring in women doctors, engineers, chemists, electricians, contractors, truck drivers, architects, and other careers that are traditionally male-dominated careers.

Learning Disability

Schools are seeing higher numbers of students with special learning disabilities than they have ever seen before. This provides schools with a responsibility to meet these learning needs and support all students as they find success.

- Partnership: It is key to solicit parent collaboration. This helps to reinforce the learning that took place at school in the home.
- Inclusion: Program intentionally and nurture a co-teaching philosophy that creates a truly collaborative partnership. Work hard to ensure the special education teacher has equal opportunity to plan and teach the class. Remember, strategies that help students with learning disabilities are often strategies that help all struggling learners in the room.
- Varied Assessments: Allow multiple ways for students to demonstrate their understanding of the learning goal(s). Like strong co-teaching, this is an approach that will help many regular education students in the classroom as well.

In addition to the groups above, we cannot forget students who have parents in prison, ones that struggle with the death of a close family member, those who are struggling with a crippling disease, and students who have an apparent insurmountable obstacle. In 2010, 2.7 million children in the United States had a parent in jail or prison. That represents about 1 in 28 minors, or nearly twice as many children as there are in the entire state of Wisconsin (Morgridge Center for Public Service, 2014). These children come under greater risk of incarceration themselves and understandably struggle in school because of additional stress in their lives. Studies show parental incarceration can be more traumatic to students than even a parent's death or divorce (Sparks, 2015). Despite its severity, this issue is often a hidden problem at school because it's hard to track and embarrassing to discuss. Additionally, the problem has a disproportionate effect on poor and minority students who are already at a disadvantage. In fact, two authors found that "one quarter of black children born in 1990 had a parent in jail or prison by the time the child was age 14, more than double the rate for black children born in 1978" (Sparks, 2015).

Perhaps one of the greatest challenges of this century will be the impact of mental health on our school system. More and more, students of all ages are coming to school with mental health issues, which many schools are not prepared to support. It's essential that school leaders learn about mental health, how to support students and families that suffer with mental health issues, and provide resources to families to get help. Work with your school counselors, medical agencies, community counseling services, ministerial groups, and businesses to find resources in your community to aid these students and families. As we strive to be future focused school leaders, we need to be aware and equipped to confront mental health challenges as they come upon us.

Relevance is key as a future focused school leader. We must change to meet the growing needs of our students and their families. We need to be ready to stretch thinking, challenge the status quo, and make brave decisions that are required to support every student. School leaders need to constantly remind the adults in your school that these students are *our* students.

RETURNING TO THE CALL

We like to ask the following question during teacher interviews: "Why do you want to be an educator?" Almost 100% of the time, educators respond the exact same way: to make a difference in the lives of students. This is more than a trite response to a common question; this is the heart of our calling as caretakers of future generations. We need to rise above the public discourse that treats education as a secondary concern and remember the privilege and responsibility that comes with being a child's mentor for the majority of their formative years.

Making a difference, which inspires others to greatness, needs to be manageable, inspiring, and invigorating. School leaders need to know that they can do this important work; it is not an elusive, visionary dream only achieved by award-winning school leaders. This must be manageable for every principal to achieve and implement immediately into their school. Our students need school leaders that can invigorate them, their teachers, and their families to achieve greatness. Here are some ways to make a sustaining difference in your school for every student:

Make It Personal

Whether you are a school leader of a school of 250 or 2,500, it's vital to the health of your school to break into small communities within your school. Create teams within grade levels, host homerooms where students meet together for all years while in that school, or use the academy system to create smaller groups within the school. Whichever strategy you choose, the important piece is to go smaller; this allows students to be known by name by several adults, build strong relationships with their peers, and develop camaraderie.

After attending the Ron Clark Academy, Robbins came back to his school and led his staff through an activity that would focus on the whole child and helping each student feel connected and supported in his school. Robbins shares, "During a Professional Development Day, I had a pic of every student on a sheet of paper with white space around the picture and I asked the teachers to write what motivates the students, what hardships they are facing, and something that interests each student." Every child in all grades had to be written about so every child's story could be told. The pictures with the writings on them were hung throughout the room and the staff did a gallery walk, viewing the postings and learning about the lives of students.

Call Students

So many school leaders shy away from this because they say there is no way they can learn the name of every student in their school. This is the wrong mentality; it's about knowing the name of the student in front of you while you walk down the hall, the one that you meet in the cafeteria, or the student that is presenting in class. Don't be shy—if you don't know their name, ask them. Stop and have a conversation with them and ask how their school day is going and what they like most about the school. As a young principal, I would hang the pictures and names of the incoming grade in my office so I could work on learning their names.

The Dot Project

Dr. Kenneth Ginsburg is a pediatrician specializing in adolescent medicine at the Children's Hospital of Philadelphia and a professor of pediatrics at the University of Pennsylvania School of Medicine. He is a leading expert on resilience in the lives of adolescent children, and author of several books on resilience for teens. He recommends an exercise for schools called the

Dot Project (Ginsburg, 2015). The goal of this project is to assure that every child in school has at least one caring adult who knows about them and can talk about their life. The project begins with a student roster of the school being hung in the faculty room, or other appropriate space. After the roster is hung staff members (teachers, aides, custodians, *all* staff) are asked to take the next few weeks and review student names. When they see a student they know they ask themselves this simple question, "Would I know if this student is having a bad day?" If they cannot answer that question with a resounding "Yes," they need to place a dot after the student's name. The dots become a strong visual reminder that there are students at risk because no adult knows them deeply, welcomes them, encourages them, pushes them, and connects them to our larger learning community. Staff members are encouraged to make strong connections with students who "have a dot" next to their name. Share pictures of these students with staff members and encourage everyone to learn more about these young lives. Dots can be key data for an advisory program, guidance staff, mentor initiative, interdisciplinary team, or extracurricular staff to use in their work with students at all grade levels. We all need to be connected to succeed.

School Leader's Story
Community Members Inspiring Students

Leader: Hayet Woods
School: Symington Elementary School
Website: http://www.hickmanmills.org/Domain/16
Setting: Urban
Size: 370 students
Grades: 1–6
Population: 80% African American, 10% Hispanic, 10% multiracial
Poverty: 100% free and reduced-price lunch
District: Hickman Mills C-1
Location: Kansas City, MO

Photo courtesy of Hayet Woods

Dr. Hayet Woods reflects, "Modeling as many positive strategies, forms of communication, celebration, etcetera, is what we must do as leaders and finding the time to do something special daily is a goal!"

Symington has a one-to-one initiative and was honored to be chosen to receive the Apple and Connect Ed grant that provided all students with their own iPad. Having their own devices allows students to have a more interactive and individualized learning environment. Students will use new technology to show their learning in various ways and enable them with the technological skills needed to succeed in future education and career choices.

In addition to an iPad for each child and staff member, each classroom has an Apple TV, projector, and SMART Board. Symington has a room where students can create media and plans to expand resources with a green screen and 3D printer this year. Dr. Woods notes, "We have to make learning relevant to our students and as highly engaging as humanly possible."

Dr. Woods holds multiple parent nights and partners with the community regularly for school events. Bringing innovative ways for our students to have mentors has birthed the latest innovation, digital mentoring! Students have the ability to FaceTime/Skype with a mentor and this allows our students to have access to mentors who may work during the day and not be able to come in during school hours frequently. More mentors can make a difference in the lives of students. This technology helps a relationship form during time spent reading together, working on school tasks, and talking about life issues.

All of these new learning opportunities will give Symington students an educational experience to prepare them for the bright futures ahead of them. Dr. Woods invites the community to support Symington students in all they can accomplish. Mentoring opportunities will help engage every student in gaining and applying new knowledge in many different ways. The commitment to new learning journeys, and the possibilities they bring, excites staff members, leaders, students, and the community.

Key Chapter Takeaways

We've offered lots of suggestions through this chapter; remember to make them your own. Future focused school leaders inspire their learning community in a style that matches their own personality, experiences, and style. Be inspired by the actions of others and consider your students, parents, and community. What will your next steps be? To help the process we encourage you to find a trusted colleague and spend a few minutes asking and answering these two simple questions: "What got you into education?" and "What keeps you there?" Take two or three minutes to quietly listen to your colleague's answer and then share your responses as they listen. After each of you has shared, the next conversation may continue for minutes, hours, or be embedded over contacts in the ensuing months.

In the rapid-fire, daily experiences of angry constituents, emotional students, urgent deadlines, unexpected emergencies, and other "important distractions," we can easily lose sight of the bigger picture. Whether we remember it or not, we are influencing the lives of our students and changing their trajectory into the world. Pull out a couple of those notes you saved from former students and parents. You know the ones we're talking about, because we usually only have a few. If you've been in education for any length of time you have probably heard from a student who matured, changed direction, and realized it wasn't the math, science, writing, or athletics that made the biggest difference. It was simply that you took the time to know them, see the best in them, not let them get away with mediocre, and mostly just listened and cared for them. Years, or decades, later the very students we inspired end up inspiring us—and future focused school leaders ensure this cycle continues.

RELATE, INNOVATE, INVIGORATE ACTIVITIES

Relate

- Write a letter, create a video message, or record a podcast message to your students.
- Lead the DOT Project in your school.
- Include a Faculty Feature in your newsletter and highlight a different staff member each time. Share their professional experiences, but also their hobbies, interests, and family life.

Innovate

- Start a schoolwide blog where all members of the community can contribute to the conversation.
- Create a Remind Group that communicates in a different language using the Translate feature.
- Start a Genius Hour in your school; set aside time for innovation and creativity. Consider starting with a student-interest survey to establish a focus for the Genius Hour.

Invigorate

- Use window glass or marker boards for students to write inspirational messages throughout the school. Start a school conversation by having students finish this phrase, "One thing I would like to invent is . . ." or "My hero is . . ."

- Finish this statement by writing and drawing a picture to hang in your office: "Future focused school leaders . . ." Be sure to share this with us and your staff. We would love to feature your story in a Future Focused post.
- Create a Google form and encourage students and parents to write a note to your teachers thanking them for their work and investment in students' lives. Share the results with your faculty, staff, administrators, and community.

Team Talk

Team Talk Stories is a conversation space for school leadership teams to share their stories from experiences with the Team Talk activities at the end of each chapter. Visit **www.chaselearning.org/TeamTalk**.

Genius Hour isn't just for students. Set aside 20% of your leadership team time for a month and see what your group produces. Like Google, you may find that some of your best ideas emerge from this less-structured time together. Pursue an audacious change your leadership team is energized about.

Continue the conversation with us on Twitter at #chaselearning.

Building on Strengths

Leadership That Focuses on Strengths and Celebrates the Success of Others

"The strength of the team is each individual member. The strength of each member is the team."

—Phil Jackson

Creating a strong leadership team and being willing to submit to each other's strengths is a strategy for organizational success. We will highlight examples of this kind of leadership. Too often leaders are evaluated on how they "strengthen their weaknesses" and valuable energy is sapped while leaders are forced to ignore what they do best. Gaps are important to fill, but building on strengths will be a superior model to bring success, and a renewed energy to the complex work of leading well. We provide school leaders key ways to build on their strengths, celebrate the success of others, and foster a school leadership team to make a sustainable difference in the life of their students.

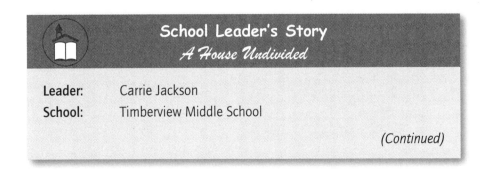

School Leader's Story
A House Undivided

Leader:	Carrie Jackson
School:	Timberview Middle School

(Continued)

(Continued)

Website: http://campus.kellerisd.net/school/tms-046

Setting: Suburban

Size: 1,225 students

Grades: 5–8

Population: 58% white, 16% Hispanic, 11% African American, 10% Asian, 5% other

Poverty: 16% economically disadvantaged

District: Keller Independent School District

Location: Fort Worth, TX

Photo courtesy of Carrie Jackson

Anyone who walks on the Timberview Middle School (TMS) Campus (home of the Hawks) can feel the energy just bursting from the hallways. This is a school that truly cares deeply for its students, that likes to have fun in learning, and that works hard to make every student feel connected to a caring adult. School leader Carrie Jackson shares, "Our entire campus—students and all staff—has been magically sorted into one of four Schoolwide houses. Each house has a name, color, and crest. Students and staff within each house have also established hand signals, chants, and other things that make the house unique. Once a student or staff member has been sorted into a house, that is his or her house forever. New students and staff are sorted into the house the day they set foot on campus. They get a house dog tag and house T-shirt, and they have a family within the greater Timberview Family with which they identify from Day One. House pride is a big deal at TMS. We have House Colors days during which students and staff go all-out dressing in their house colors. We have house activity days during which students and staff participate in contests to earn house points. Houses earn house points throughout the year for things like initiating and participating in service work, performing good deeds, showing up to support performances and sports, winning contests, and so on. The house with the greatest number of points at the end of the year wins the House Cup and gets a special celebration. We have a student president and vice president for each house, and we have teacher mentors for each house. We have found that the key element of a successful house is outrageously supportive and enthusiastic staff."

Another big piece of TMS is Best First Day Ever! Jackson works to build on the strengths of her faculty and staff, and to celebrate the success of them and her students. She is energized by seeing others win and succeed.

Principal Jackson shares, "Best First Day Ever: Timberview goes all-out on the first day of school. Our leadership team selects a theme during the summer, and we keep the theme a secret from the kids and parents. We have a purple carpet (school colors) greeting for students on the first day of school, with staff in costume. For example, last year staff dressed in formal attire and we had a movie star/celebrity theme; this year we dressed as superheroes and carried the theme 'What is *your* superpower?' We pump loud music into the main entrance and the cafeteria area and make it a big party. We want the kids to know we are *so* happy to have them back! Parents are welcome to come in and take all the pictures they want. The parents often get as big a kick out of it as the kids. Once the kids get into the building we whisk them off to a surprise assembly. For example, one year we had a glow in the dark dance party. This year we brought in the Drum Cafe. Every student had a drum and participated in a fun and interactive character lesson to music. We sort new students into houses on the first day, do team-building activities, help orient the kids to campus, and focus on relationships. We end the day with a schoolwide pep rally to encourage house unity and also unity across the entire campus. The pep rally comes with surprises from the staff as well. This year it was a whole-staff—about 130 adults—Stomp routine and a fierce game of teacher Bubble Soccer. The goal—pardon the pun—is to make the day memorable for kids. Another key strategy is we 'break' our social media channels posting photos and videos so the parents can live it out from work or home. This is crucial to building parent/family trust and relationships."

THE POWER OF TEAM

If you're leading a school by yourself, you are working with a limited set of skills and strengths. If you are leading with a team, you may be no better off. That sounds harsh, but some leaders want their team to be mini-me clones instead of a diverse group of leadership contributors. To maximize the power of your team you need to know each other (relationships again!) and more specifically, you need to know each team member's strengths. To work well as a team, it's helpful to know one other key item: your own weaknesses. If you are the leader with "the power" who knows yourself well (weaknesses), knows your team well (their strengths), and you're willing to submit and share your power, you have a recipe for success!

This approach is not the same as servant leadership. A servant leader can still have a Superman complex and try to do all the leading, and serving, themselves. You may really want to be a leader who leads with a team, but how does aspiration turn to operation? Here's an idea to build your leadership team success: Next time your team gathers put the pressing problem du jour aside and consider a CPO strategy (discussed in Chapter 1) similar to this:

- Context: With all the challenges we face as a school, it's more important than ever to lead well together.
- Purpose: Today we are going to build a stronger team by learning more about what each of us does well.
- Outcome: After learning each other's strengths, skills, and passions, we will create solutions together by using the best resources our team has to offer.

You could start right after your CPO announcement with a short activity to unpack the gifts that each team member brings to the table. People often struggle with the questions, "What is your greatest strength?" and "What is your biggest weakness?" Sometimes people can answer one easily but struggle with the other. We recommend using the question with a twist. Next are two options to gather the same data.

The Pragmatic Way

Ask each person to get a sheet of paper or digital document ready. Place the name of each person on your leadership team on the document. Now consider that person and write a strength they bring to the team next to their name. See if you can find two or three for each person. Don't over analyze; go with the trait that comes to mind first. For example, "Jenna is a strong problem solver," "Javier always looks out for students," "Jon is very detail oriented," or "Janice can always come up with an idea that no one else has thought of." After five or 10 minutes of individual reflection bring the sheets together and look for commonality of responses. Where the alignment occurs you have a pretty good confirmation of some personal strengths for your team member.

The Invigorating Way

This is one of our three main tenets! Do the same individual identifying of strengths, and the analysis of people's responses at the end of the data gathering. The big difference is how you gather the input from each team member. Instead of a paper/document in front of each team member as they sit quietly and ponder, you start with a physical sheet of paper that each person writes their own name on (at the top). If you want to sit at the table, you can begin to circulate the papers so that every person eventually lists strengths for the person on the sheet with their name on top. If you want a more active way to gather data, take the sheet of paper and tape it to the person's back. Now your team can go around the room and write a strength or two on the paper, while it's taped to the back of the person they are "complimenting." They can even use sticky notes to post on the person's back and then use the app Post-it Plus to collect all of the sticky notes electronically.

Whatever your data-gathering approach, you end up with characteristics of each team member that are not only energizing to each individual, but you provide a starting point to compliment the leader's weaknesses and build the capacity of your team! Part of the definition of the word *invigorate* is to provide more energy; and discovering, then submitting, to each other's strengths is a great way to energize the work.

FOCUS ON STRENGTHS

As school leaders we can be very critical, often most critical of our own performance. Moving forward, let's focus on what we are good at, what comes naturally, and growing the skills that we are best at. Why continue to strengthen our weaknesses? Now, we aren't saying avoiding our weaknesses altogether, but we are saying we should place more energy, time, and effort into building on our strengths.

What are you good at? Maybe you are an organizer, a great communicator, a systems thinker, a motivator, an innovator, or a problem solver. But there's a good chance you aren't strong in all of these areas. So, rather than trying constantly throughout your entire life to get better at what you are weak at, focus on your strengths. Become the best organizer, communicator, systems thinker, motivator, innovator, or problem solver your school has ever seen.

The important piece is to surround yourself with people who complement you as a leader. Don't forget to take the risk and include teacher leaders as people you give power to (Ziegler & Ramage, 2012). Your leadership team should have strengths where you are weak and vice versa. This allows others to use their giftedness, and it creates a team approach to thinking and doing. Plus, it frees you up to do what you love! When you are able to focus on what you love, what you thrive on, what you were born to do, then you are empowered and equipped with the opportunity to make systemic and meaningful growth for your students, teachers, parents, and community.

I want you to know that this journey to focus on your strengths will not come easy; other leaders and your critics will continue to point out your areas of weakness and try to sap your energy by getting you to work to improve in that area. However, don't listen to your critics; stay focused on the strengths and allow others to use their skills to complement your leadership. This is the true representation of a highly functional team. Think about it: If the center on a football team kept learning how to catch a ball because that was one of his weaknesses, he would never find time to learn how to snap the ball. The same is true with you; find what you are good at, build on that, and allow others to come alongside you to complement your leadership.

Crowdsourcing is revolutionizing the way entrepreneurship and venture capital work. Take a similar approach by "crowdsolving" your next big problem or challenge at school. Don't limit the work to a small group of school leaders who hold all the final decision-making power. You can gain a lot of wisdom and knowledge just by expanding the decision-making power to your existing organization and community. Going a step further to include professional learning networks (PLN) will only bolster the quality of your final outcome.

Teacher Leaders

Flattening an organization's hierarchy has been shown to produce many benefits for the organization. There are many ways to "flatten" an organization. Starbucks is unconventional in the way they embed surprise in their structures and practices. They promoted a flattening of salary structures in 2004 by giving holiday bonuses to lower-level employees who met basic criteria, like worked 500 hours in the year. Each of the qualifying workers received a surprise $250 holiday bonus. "This bonus was not for the store managers and above; rather, it was for the baristas and shift supervisors" (Michelli, 2007 p. 93). Instead of flattening compensation, Google flattens time by offering 20% of the workweek for employees or teams to develop their own ideas. Some of Google's most popular services were born from this 20% time. In *The Eight Pillars of Innovation*, Google founders Larry Page and Sergey Brin note, "We try to encourage this type of blue-sky thinking through '20 percent time'—a full day a week during which engineers can work on whatever they want. Looking back at our launch calendar over a recent six-month period, we found that many products started life in employees' 20 percent time" (Wojcick, 2011).

You may have little influence over compensation or time, but consider flattening your organization by giving away decisions. We know this works well in a classroom setting. We've all witnessed the power of a classroom where a teacher has stepped aside and shared power with their students. The engagement and motivation in that kind of learning environment is impressive. Despite our experience as classroom observers, many building and/or system leaders fail to share power and flatten their organization in a similar way.

Strategies like Twitter Takeover Day, student-led conferences, and student-led professional development provide ways to share power. Empowering students is important; however, committing to minimize "solo decisions" is even more powerful. Collaborating with an administrative partner, guidance team, or cabinet is a good start, but whenever possible share decision-making power with a broad base of constituents including teachers, students, and community members. The synergy of collaboration with a large portion of your organization allows a variety of individual strengths to help you produce effective solutions.

Collaborative Leadership

Whether you lead a school alone or if you have a large team to lead the school along with you, empowering others breathes life into the school and builds leadership capacity. It's important to build a core leadership team you can rely on and partner with in moving the school forward. We call this team our School Leadership Team. Team Talk activities ending each chapter are designed to support this team.

If you are the only school leader, be sure to bring a core leadership team around you to support your leadership in the building. Assign tasks according to teacher strengths and delegate responsibilities to help get the work done. Be sure to bring the leadership team together weekly to review the week ahead, examine important school events, and reflect on the effectiveness of the team.

If you are a school leader who has several other school leaders around you, it's just as important to develop a core leadership team that focuses on the same items above. The nice opportunity for this type of school is that each school leader can be assigned a team to lead. One team can focus on school management, another curriculum and assessment, another on school safety, and so on. Empower the leaders alongside you and be sure to regularly meet to discuss goals, current updates, and other important information.

We like to keep all of our School Leadership Team notes in Schoology, or others use Google to store them. This allows team members to review the notes if they were absent, and it also allows you to monitor the progress of the team. Plus, we model digital leadership in these meetings and encourage the team members to do the same.

Collaborative leadership relies on the leaders in the School Leadership Team to update other staff members in the school. This avoids constantly having faculty meetings for items and things that can be discussed in smaller groups by the team leader. For instance, after you share an important update about upcoming teacher observations, have the Grade 3 level team leader share this information with all the Grade 3 teachers. When school leaders empower their teacher leaders, they expand the leadership capacity in the school and provide opportunities for others to use their leadership skill set to serve students.

Establish Team Norms

When School Leadership Teams establish norms, team members know what to expect and how to act, lead, and think. Plus, it models what you want to see from teachers and students in the classroom.

What can a school leader do when a team member does not reflect the values of the school and team? Don't ignore it! This will most likely not go away, and it will only begin to deteriorate the culture of the leadership team and your school. Leaders tend to shy away from conflict of this type. Lean into the wind and talk to the person as we outline below.

- Honest Talk: Have an honest conversation with the team member. Focus on observations and the school's core values. Shy away from giving your opinion, and stick to the facts. You can say, "Your late arrivals to meetings goes against our team norm of respecting others with time." Make sure you review expectations to be a School Leadership Team member and ask the person if they would like to continue in this role. Who knows, they may want out and don't know how to get out of it. Just by giving them the opportunity, they may decide serving on the team is not for them.
- Give It Time: Change doesn't happen overnight; respect the team and allow them time to reflect and make change. This isn't easy, and it can be a slow process; be patient but set clear expectations.
- Provide Support: Support team members and search for ways to strengthen them and their teaching. By doing this, you model the respect that your team values most.
- Team Meeting: Ask a team member to join you in talking to this team member. Host this meeting in your office and inquire on how the team member is doing and how you have not observed a change in the behavior. Set a timeline that so that the team member knows what to expect, recognizes how to get supports, and understands the exit plan from the School Leadership Team.

Make time for the core leadership team to learn together. Doing a book study, attending professional development together, or simply watching a series of TED Talk videos and reflecting on them together is a valuable way to learn and grow. Use this book to work through the Team Talk activities at the end of each chapter and learn together. Focus your learning to align with your school goals, school improvement plan, and mission. Find something to stretch your team to become stronger leaders. Learning about leadership is key to develop the leadership capacity and skill set of your team leaders. There should be a balance between learning about learning and your school's goals and leadership. Encourage your team leaders to showcase their work and leadership in the school. Have them lead a faculty meeting, write a newsletter to parents, lead a grade-level planning session, and work to strengthen personalized learning in the school. Count on these leaders to use what they are learning not just in the team but in their classrooms, faculty room discussions, and hallway conversations.

Celebrate Success

Implementing a system to recognize the contributions of staff members can really boost the climate and culture of your school. Having a simple form, or other process, to allow staff members to nominate peers for recognition helps you honor staff members' contributions and shares power at the same time. Many schools are beginning to join an established effort like "Thanks A Latte" at www.chaselearning.org/resources to celebrate successes and offer a small thank you for staff.

These celebrations mirror a research-based approach to student discipline known as School-Wide Positive Behavior Systems (SWPBS), or Positive Behavior Interventions and Supports (PBIS; see www.chaselearning.org/resources). These frameworks echo what we are proposing: celebrating the kinds of actions we want to see over and over again. Celebrating successes helps breed further success. Do this frequently with a method that fits your school culture and you will begin to celebrate the strengths of your staff. If building relationships with students is important (and we definitely think it is) then you can give a Thanks-A-Latte card to a staff member who's connecting with students. This raises the likelihood of that behavior happening again and celebrates the strengths of your staff. Tap into local businesses for coffee, pizza, or ice cream gift card prizes, and you're also creating partnerships with community stakeholders. All this is directed at the goal of students' academic and emotional success. Some of the most successful attempts we've seen in this type of celebration is when teachers give away the Thanks-A-Latte cards too. This shows we're all in this together and ensures the reinforcement of culture is not limited to the building administration team.

School Leader's Story
Stronger Together: Collaborating for Success

Leader: Bill Truesdale

School: Douglas Taylor Elementary School

Website: http://taylor.cps.edu

Setting: Urban

Size: 507 students

Grades: PreK–8

Population: 89% Hispanic, 8% African American, 3% other

Poverty: 98% economically disadvantaged

District: Chicago Public School District

Location: Chicago, IL

Photo courtesy of Bill Truesdale

Dr. Bill Truesdale believes strongly in the strategy of collaborative leadership. He shared that he uses collaborative leadership to bring the teachers together to develop incentives, conduct student home visits, and to make regular phone calls home to students. His team actually charts its progress on a visual chart that hangs in an area that all teachers and staff members can see on a regular basis. Through his staff's hard work and dedication to connect with every student, the school's daily attendance is 96.04%, one of the highest in the large district. Dr. Truesdale and his team are regularly celebrating the work of students and are intent in making every student feel valued, connected to an adult, and as a key member of the school.

Dr. Truesdale shares, "We also participated in the United States Department of Education's College Sign Up Day on April 26. This is a day where we had our elementary school students sign a school banner promising that they would go to college and all of the faculty wore their college gear on this special day."

With collaborative leadership, Taylor's comprehensive plan is broken into five categories and teachers select two areas of the comprehensive plan that they would like to contribute to. This empowers the staff and uses their strengths and expertise to move the school forward.

Dr. Truesdale and his team believe that the expertise needed to move his school forward is not some educational expert that will cost thousands, but the teacher right across the hall. That's right: Teachers at Taylor Elementary do peer walkthroughs to learn from their peers and they use a tool called, "My Best Ideas Sheet" to use when learning from teachers while in their classroom; they write down best ideas and this gets shared with the staff. Dr. Truesdale is using the skills of his teachers to strengthen the teaching and learning in his school.

The Three Bs reign at Taylor: Be Responsible, Be Respectful, and Be at Your Best! Students learn about the positive behavior support program the first three days of school, receiving lessons on how to be responsible, respectful, and how to be their best. Dr. Truesdale relies on his teachers' strengths to nurture the growth of this positive behavior support plan, and it has dramatically increased positive behaviors in the school. When we teach the best, expect the best, we often get the best from students.

Key Chapter Takeaways

You can encourage energy and innovation in your organization by allowing the strengths of your individual staff members to flourish. Harness the power of your organization's strengths instead of focusing on deficits and weaknesses. Crowdsourcing sites like Kickstarter or GoFundMe are revolutionizing venture capital; consider "crowdsolving" your next big challenge by engaging your whole organization and community to use the strengths that are already in place. Give away some of your decision power and the results may astound you. Giving away communication power is at the heart of a Twitter Takeover Day. Find a staff member or student who will tell a part of your school's story and it's likely to be more powerful than you ever imagined.

RELATE, INNOVATE, INVIGORATE ACTIVITIES

Relate

- Form a School Leadership Team and have the team focus on your school's strengths.
- Collaborate with your School Leadership Team to establish norms, expectations, and goals.
- Create a course in your learning management system for your faculty/staff. Include a section for staff members to share their instructional practices through short posts, pictures, and videos.

Innovate

- Showcase a teacher or student on social media and feature the learning.

- Host a book study using Voxer to share reflections, to learn, and grow together.
- Host a Teacher Twitter Takeover Day to feature the day in the life of a teacher.

Invigorate

- Celebrate the accomplishments and hard work of your staff today. Send them a text or Remind message to encourage and celebrate.
- Write a handwritten note thanking a staff member, student, or parent and send it to their house via mail.
- Call or meet with your staff member, student, or parent to share how much you appreciate the work they are doing, what they are good at, and how they are invaluable to your school.

Team Talk

Team Talk Stories is a conversation space for School Leadership Teams to share their stories from experiences with the Team Talk activities at the end of each chapter; visit **www.chaselearning.org/TeamTalk.**

Post your Storify archive, Facebook Live session, or other social media takeover event at the Team Talk link and see what other school leaders are doing to highlight the strengths of their schools.

Continue the conversation with us on Twitter at #chaselearning.

Servant Leadership

Serving the Students, Staff, and Community to Ensure They Get What They Need to Learn

"True leadership must be for the benefit of the followers, not to enrich the leader."

—John C. Maxwell

"Servant-leadership is all about making the goals clear and then rolling your sleeves up and doing whatever it takes to help people win. In that situation, they don't work for you, you work for them."

—Ken Blanchard

T his chapter explores the role of power, and the giving away of power, as a key element in leadership success. Stories of leaders sharing power, and the powerful outcome, will both inspire leaders and offer practical strategies to imitate in their organizations. Readers will come away with inspiring and practical steps to serve their school community in a way that builds on the foundations they have established within their own school.

School Leader's Story
Serving the School Community

Leader: James Orichosky

School: Wingate Elementary School

Website: www.beasd.org

Setting: Rural

Size: 500 students

Grades: K–5

Population: 94.0% white, 2.0% Hispanic, 2.0% black, 1.3% multiracial, 0.6% Asian, 0.1% Native American

Poverty: 43.85% economically disadvantaged

District: Bald Eagle Area School District

Location: Wingate, PA

Photo courtesy of James Orichosky

There is nothing better to invigorate a faculty and staff than to give them a chance to give back to their students. Principal Jim Orichosky is doing just that. Every Thursday, Orichosky, his faculty, staff, and members of the YMCA of Centre County partner together to make sure every child has food over the weekend. Orichosky and his team understand that students cannot learn well if their basic needs are not being met. He and his team go beyond the call of duty to serve their students. They exemplify true servant leadership. They live out the words of Mother Theresa who reminds us, "At the end of life we will not be judged by how many diplomas we have received, how much money we have made, how many great things we have done. We will be judged by 'I was hungry, and you gave me something to eat, I was naked and you clothed me. I was homeless, and you took me in.'"

Orichosky explains, "the weekend backpack program is a partnership between the YMCA of Centre County and Bald Eagle Area School District. The focus behind this program is to provide opportunities for families in the school district and to help fight childhood hunger. Each Thursday evening a group of volunteers gather together at Wingate Elementary School and fill backpacks with food for students to take home for the weekend. Currently the Wingate Elementary fill station is providing over 200 backpacks for students in two area school districts. As principal of Wingate Elementary, I am quite proud to serve as host school for this program. The partnership between the YMCA of Centre County and the Bald Eagle Area School District is one of the great benefits for the members of this community. The backpack program is helping students with a basic need and fighting childhood hunger. I look forward to this program expanding and helping as many students as possible in the future."

Sharing Power or Collaborative Leadership

Schools must be learning organizations, but learning does not happen automatically. Visiting classrooms, reviewing student work, collecting artifacts, and analyzing achievement data are essential to the health of a school and its ability to educate students. Leaders must intentionally shift the expectations of typical teacher–leader opportunities to foster a higher investment among teachers. The only way to make transformational changes is for teachers, administrators, and staff members to do the work together. Sharing leadership and sharing power is a risk at every level of the school. Students risk ridicule when they seek help for understanding, teachers risk chaos when they give away the learning, and principals risk improvements that quickly disappear—if each group fails to share the ownership of learning. Thankfully, educators can make progress by moving ahead together.

KINDERGARTEN LESSONS

Ironically, we can gain a great deal of insight by returning to the earliest stages of our own formal education. When 5-year-olds come together to form a learning community we instinctively know a large portion of the work will require us to move each student from an individual mindset to a community mindset. You could argue that the shift is equally important for all school leaders—because the tendency is similar. Put too much stock in your own personal abilities and power, and you will never bring about the full potential of your learning organization. We can learn by returning to some key "kindergarten principles": Everyone needs a buddy, it's good to share, we need to help each other, tell the truth, recess is important, and clean up your mess.

Everyone Needs a Buddy

Real School Leaders Don't Fly Solo

Without a doubt, we would have never made it as school leaders if we didn't have colleagues that we could reach out to for support. These lifelines are critical for every school leader to have a sustaining and successful career as a school leader. Leaders need to be intentional in making the work collaborative and collegial.

We may still have relationships with our initial mentors; most likely we have others we rely on now for feedback. Are you actively seeking a leader that you can mentor? This is a shared process, not merely an "expert" and a "novice" relationship. We encourage all school leaders to have three other school leaders in their life that are part of the cycle of mentoring. Three stages of mentoring help to keep the cycle of healthy leadership vibrant and strong.

New Leader School leaders should be working to mentor, guide, and coach a younger school leader. These relationships can also stretch the more seasoned school leader because these younger leaders often see life and leadership from a fresh perspective. Many times, they are innovative, tech savvy, and risk takers. But they also are hungry for someone to mentor and guide them along the journey of being a school leader. When mentoring, it's important to not act as the expert but as one who has years of experience, knowledge, history, and perspective that only comes through time. Make a commitment to check in with this new leader regularly and schedule times that can be longer discussion times to work through real-life problems. Be available at a moment's notice either in person, phone, text, or video conferencing to assist the new leader when they face a challenge that seems insurmountable, want to run an "Aha!" moment by you, or they need someone to listen after a hard day.

Peer Leader We highly value our peer leader colleagues who extend our collaborative leadership and provide rich and regular opportunities to plan, practice, and dream together. You may naturally find peer leaders in your organization; consider reaching peers outside your own organization. We have grown immensely through our work with school leader associations such as the National Association of Elementary School Principals, the National Association of Secondary School Principals, and their state affiliates. These connections happen often on social media such as Twitter, Voxer, Facebook, and Google Hangouts, but they also thrive over lunch together, connecting after work, or even during the work day.

Veteran Leader It's important that all leaders have someone they are being mentored, coached, and guided by. Many times, these are leaders who are older or more seasoned than us. They could be retired leaders from a similar role or leaders who are working in a different organizational level. These relationships are critical for all school leaders to grow and develop in their own practice. This mentoring model plays out over a cup of coffee, a visit to your school, or a Google Hangout, Facebook Live, or Facetime chat.

It's Good to Share: Real School Leaders Give Their Best Away

Have you ever been in the home of a hoarder? School leaders can easily become hoarders of knowledge, success, power, resources, and ideas causing their faculty, staff, students, and parents to chart a course through the choppy waters of daily life in their school. When this happens all members of the school community are harmed. School leaders need to give away their best ideas, share resources, and work to empower others. Here are some tips to give away your best:

- Share With Every School in Your System: Too often, school leaders, especially those who have similar schools in their organization, try to keep the best practices to themselves so they look better or have higher scores. Share and collaborate with other school leaders.

> *"Some may see them as the crazy ones; we see genius, because the ones who are crazy enough to think that they can change the world are the ones who do."*

- Social Media: Our world has a shortage of great, creative, and innovative ideas for school leaders. Share your ideas with the world by posting them on social media and keep the learning going.
- Blog Post: Create your own blog to share what works best for you. We would love to feature your blog post and celebrate the great work with you.
- Future Focused School Leaders: Please share your great ideas, successes, and resources with us so we can feature you on our website. We want to hear what's working for you, and share what's working for other school leaders by going to www.chaselearning.org.

When a school leader gives away his or her best ideas and success, it causes them to continue to come up with new, fresh, and innovative ideas to share within the organization. Plus, it empowers others to be leaders and to think differently for the best of students. It's time to surrender power and control and focus on empowering others.

We Help Each Other: Real School Leaders Dumpster Dive!

Have you ever gone dumpster diving as a school leader? Both of us have proudly jumped into the mess to rescue a retainer, cell phone, or other item mistaken for trash in the midst of a busy lunch period. What does dumpster diving have to do with leadership? It demonstrates a leader's willingness to be selfless and consider the needs of others first. We don't look forward to dumpster diving, but we would both do it again whenever the situation arises.

We need other leaders (as mentioned in the mentoring ideas above), but leaders need more than fellow leaders to be successful. One big reason this principle breeds success is because we generate better ideas and solutions together. Have you ever considered where you can find the best ideas in your organization? If a few key people, probably leaders, come to mind you may be missing a critical aspect of how systems work. Ken Blanchard and others have said, "None of us is as smart as all of us," and this axiom is true. Knowledge is shared through an organization; it does not reside in one or two key individuals. If you are trying to be that one repository of knowledge you are placing unnecessary pressure on yourself! Worst of all, you are withholding the best possible solutions from your students, staff, and families. When you're working together, your organization has a wealth of knowledge and resources. We need each other to be at our best.

Part of being at our best is having others in mind. We serve many students, staff, and families that have serious struggles and tragic life events. Make sure you use the relationship-building strategies and tools we highlight in the book to support each other as life unfolds. Attending the funeral services for a coworker's parents, spouse, or child can speak volumes about your authentic care for one another. Listening to a student or staff member, really listening, so they feel heard is an amazing way to show you care about them. You hear leaders say, "I serve as principal for . . ." I serve as superintendent of . . ." but do their daily routines demonstrate the value of service? How do your routines speak to serving others? This is a tough question that all of us could benefit from considering on a regular basis. Pick up trash as you walk through your campus, hold the hallway door open for students, write a thank-you note to a person who worked behind the scenes for a school success, and pitch in to help with the least glamorous aspects of your school's daily routines.

Tell the Truth: Real School Leaders Care About Character

Kindergarten teachers teach values like honesty and respect all the time in their classes. We can learn a great deal from these simple life lessons as leaders. The character of a leader matters. You can have all the skills and abilities needed for successful leadership, but if you lack the character traits it will be difficult to influence others to follow along with you. Leaders who are focused on leading and living with character are more likely to be successful and have longer sustaining influence as school leaders. This means always telling the truth (even when it doesn't benefit you), acting the same when others aren't looking, being responsible with resources and finances, and treating others as you want to be treated. In practical terms, this also means not blaming others for your own faults, taking credit for things you didn't accomplish, or reveling in the losses of others. These may be time-tested strategies in the world of school politics, but they are not quality leadership principles. It's easy to get sucked into the vortex of negativity or pounce on an idea that wasn't yours, but take time to reflect, pause, and be encouraging in your tone, body language, words, and messaging.

Sadly, we have seen our share of school leaders who end up on the front page for the wrong thing or spiral out of control and need to leave the profession. When we lead with a character mindset, school leaders filter everything they do through the lens of integrity and character. The character mindset should be at the core of everything we do as school leaders. The character mindset believes that it doesn't matter how strong of a leader you are if you don't have character at the heart of leadership. This mindset is nurtured through discipline, regular practice, and not forgetting our moral purpose as school leaders.

This mindset flows into the leader's personal life and that is reflected in their leadership. We like to think of the character mindset as the constant voice of your kindergarten teacher whispering to you what's right or wrong and acting on that to do the right thing.

Clean Up Your Mess: Real School Leaders Fail

It's unrealistic to think you will never make a leadership mistake. But the truth is, it doesn't even require a "mistake" to cause a mess. Our kindergarten teachers reminded us to always clean up, stack our blocks, or put our toys away—and we can benefit from that same advice as school leaders. In the midst of new implementations and initiatives, curriculum discussions, assessment results, or personnel decisions, never forget to consider the people behind the decisions and pay attention to their morale. We are not advocating pandering to the masses; we need to make difficult decisions and stand by them—but we don't need to run people over in the process. Sometimes a decision leads to a course of action that has to be discontinued, or reversed. This is a time to admit we are not superheroes, listen to suggestions for revision, and build unity to move ahead for success.

Moving ahead successfully may require an apology. We can never be too proud to admit fault and apologize. Admitting responsibility for failure is a powerful way your staff, students, or families can see your moral character in action. Pushing blame to another person or team is also a way they can see your failing character. Don't be afraid to say, "I'm sorry the decision I made led to that nasty interaction with one of our families."

Recess Is Important: Real School Leaders Rest and Play

Recess was always my favorite time of the school day. It gave me a chance to play and run around with my friends and always felt like a brain break.

As school leaders, we need to make sure that we are taking a recess to rest and play. The school-issued laptop, tablet, and phone can all be reasons to resist rest and play, but everyone needs some down time.

Rest

School leaders can be so wrapped up in their leadership and school they forget to take care of themselves. It's the old flight attendant principle of putting your oxygen mask on before assisting others. The same is true with school leadership: We are regularly working to help others that we often forget about ourselves. Below are some strategies we use to gain rest, store up energy, and restore perspective:

- Sleep: I know this sounds simplistic, but sleep is the fuel you need to have a sharp and clear mind. Work to get 7–9 hours of sleep each day. A power nap is also a great way to get refreshed to go back before an evening meeting.
- Food: This probably sounds like your mom, but it's critical to eat a healthy breakfast. Wake up early enough that you can sit down and have breakfast; breakfast on the road is not the breakfast of champions for school leaders. Plus, eat healthy, make good choices, and do everything in moderation throughout the day. Make sure you get a lunch time to sit, for a few minutes, and enjoy your meal. We know this is simple to say, and often difficult to put into practice.
- Meditation/Prayer: It's important to get time away and free your mind from the unending to-do list. This time is perfect to center yourself and clear out the distractions to find peace and tranquility.
- Vacation: So many school leaders find it hard to check out from the school. But do your family and friends a favor when you go on vacation and leave the e-mails, phone, and school work back at home or at least in the hotel. Try to use vacation time as time away from school. This will recharge your batteries and empower you for more productive work when you return.

Play

Play is a broad category of activity. Just as our students are more and more likely to experience formal play in leagues moderated by adults, many school leaders find an outlet for play in established programs at health clubs, YMCAs, or community leagues. These can be terrific outlets for stress relief, but there are many opportunities for play that we can leverage inside our schools. The good news is the essence of play is very informal.

Make time in your daily, or weekly, routines to intentionally come alongside your students and staff in less formal settings. If you're a musician, grab your instrument and go to the band room or sing with the chorus. Maybe you take a funny cameo appearance in the school play or musical. If your school has a recess time join in with some students and toss a Frisbee, swing a jump rope, or kick a ball. Join the Running Man video your students are making, or hop on the dance floor during a PTA dance. You can create opportunities for play in the daily routines of changing classes, morning announcements, or loading/unloading buses. Basically, don't overlook the opportunity to have fun with your students and staff.

Whether it's taking a pie in the face, getting soaked in the dunk tank, sumo wrestling, or being taped to the wall with duct tape (all things we've done), be sure to have fun and play to raise money for your school and their favorite charity. These times become memorable events that people will talk about positively. They show your willingness to go beyond your job responsibilities to make a difference. The play opportunities we describe can help students see appropriate risk taking in action. Your play may inspire a student to stretch in their classroom setting.

Play in your own personal life can fuel you to be a stronger school leader. We believe true future focused leaders live the balance between work and play. Play as a school leader means spending quality and quantity time with your family and friends, enjoying doing what you love most, and getting energized for the week ahead. When we play, we relieve stress, ignite creativity, and get replenished to give back and lead our schools.

We also believe that future focused leaders are committed to their health and well-being. This includes scheduling time for exercise, eating healthy, and making sure you are taking care of your body.

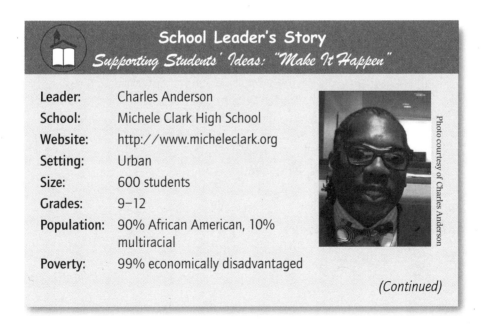

School Leader's Story
Supporting Students' Ideas: "Make It Happen"

Leader:	Charles Anderson
School:	Michele Clark High School
Website:	http://www.micheleclark.org
Setting:	Urban
Size:	600 students
Grades:	9–12
Population:	90% African American, 10% multiracial
Poverty:	99% economically disadvantaged

Photo courtesy of Charles Anderson

(Continued)

(Continued)

District: Chicago Public Schools
Location: Chicago, IL

School leader Charles Anderson is committed to serving his students and making sure they have what they need to be successful in school and life. He shares, "I listen to the students and then make them accountable for their ideas, and I challenge them to follow through on whatever their idea or goal is and then I don't box them in. I say to the kids, 'Dream Big,' so we can then make it happen. Now I say, Dream Big and now wake up to make that dream happen. They want to have more school spirit, we saw increases in attendance—one of the highest attendance rates in the city." Anderson meets monthly with students, by grade level, so they can hear his voice speaking into their lives. "I think it's important that my students know I believe in them and that they see me taking an interest in their lives."

Anderson goes on to share, "I have a couple of kids on the football team who dreamed of having a larger weight room for their team. As we got closer to the end of the budget, I brought these students together and we found a room that they turned into a weight room. That idea came from them, not me. Now that they have this room, I walk in regularly and ask how can we improve this and students give me feedback and we have grown it to other sports teams using this room. I even asked some of the students to be my trainer. These students challenge me on my eating habits and fitness on a regular basis. To the point, I sneak into my office to eat a Snickers bar so they don't see me eating it. I know they would call me out on eating this candy bar. This is pushing one of them into a career as a personal trainer."

Anderson also has a freshmen orientation in his school where he brings in the ninth graders over the summer for four weeks; every student gets a free shirt, participates in team-building activities, and even has an opportunity to earn money. Part of the orientation is to provide job skills for students and then students actually get summer jobs in the district earning money.

He is proud to share that 100% of his students attend post-secondary education and last year they received $4.6 million in scholarships. "This success is because of the hard work of our teachers and students; our teachers are committed to serving our students in a way that makes going to college a requirement for all students."

Key Chapter Takeaways

There are powerful lessons to be harvested from the social context of learning that are salient in most preschool, kindergarten, and primary classrooms. We will gain many academic, behavioral, and social-emotional benefits for students, and staff, if our secondary schools can be more like kindergarten classrooms. This is more than a trite poster to hang on our walls; it's a recognition of the social nature of learning. If you use this social context to help your school serve others in the community, or around the globe, you create a tremendously powerful synergy of learning, doing, and being that will bring success to everyone involved. The greatest school leaders are in the work to serve others.

RELATE, INNOVATE, INVIGORATE ACTIVITIES

Relate

- Find a mentor that you can look up to, learn from, and confide in. If you already have one, schedule a meeting to discuss your reflections from this chapter.
- Join together with two or three colleagues to host a book study and be sure to meet monthly.
- Find a young school leader who you can mentor. Please share your story with us so we can feature you and the young leader on our website.

Innovate

- Show Off – Showcase your school through video and/or podcasting about the great work of your students and teachers.
- Share Your Best Work – Create a blog to share your expertise and what you find is working great. Please share your blog with us so we can feature your work and learn from you.
- Go Dumpster Diving! – No, we don't mean actually dumpster diving, but focus on being selfless and giving away to others.

Invigorate

- Be Sure to Rest – Make a commitment to get plenty of rest—plus, take a nap after work or between school and your nightly meeting.
- Get Energized, Get Active – Get a Fitbit or other device and begin tracking your physical activity.
- Play – Be sure to have fun with your students and staff. Plus, be sure to play with your family and friends; this reenergizes us to be the best school leaders we can be.

Team Talk

Team Talk Stories is a conversation space for school leadership teams to share their stories from experiences with the Team Talk activities at the end of each chapter.

Your work to serve others impacts others. This sounds like a Captain Obvious quote, but we often miss the opportunity to include the "participant voice." For this chapter's Team Talk assignment, assign members of your team to do short interviews or focus groups with people in the community who have been served by your school. It's fine to include student voices, but do your best to get parents, guardians, community members, school board directors, and others. Turn your conversations into a short written piece or video documentary and share the result at the Team Talk page at **www.chaselearning.org/TeamTalk**.

Continue the conversation with us on Twitter at #chaselearning.

10

Learning Is the Goal

Leadership That Resists Trends and Quick Fixes

"Good teaching may be possible in a school in which there is weak and ineffective educational leadership, but it is harder to achieve. Change and sustained improvement are impossible without good educational leadership, particularly where whole-school change is sought."

—Fullan, Hill, & Crévola

Sustaining a leadership on learning seems like it would be second nature in a school setting, but we all know better. So many things compete for our attention and our leadership focus. We must not allow these distractions to shift our focus from the doggedly persistent pursuit of learning. The promise of technology to change learning provides our strongest lever for new practices in our field. Ironically, that technology can also become an end in itself that pulls us away from the learning goal we must maintain. We will continue to chase the learning as we inspire, equip, and engage others to do the same.

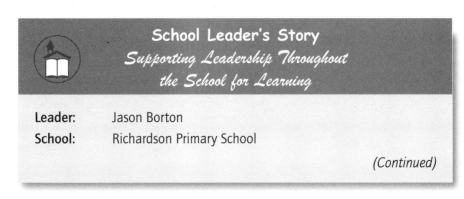

School Leader's Story
Supporting Leadership Throughout the School for Learning

Leader: Jason Borton

School: Richardson Primary School

(Continued)

(Continued)

Website:	http://www.richardsonps.act.edu.au/
Setting:	Urban
Size:	200 students
Grades:	PreK–6
Population:	Race/ethnicity not recorded; indigenous population is significant
Poverty:	Economic status is not recorded
District:	ACT Public Schools
Location:	Canberra, Australia

Photo courtesy of Jason Borton

Jason Borton, the school leader at Richardson Primary School, is an acclaimed school leader in Australia. Here are some of Borton's thoughts on school leadership:

"Coming up to my twelfth year as a school leader and almost five as a principal, I have been spending a lot of time recently thinking about what I've learned about leadership. I have developed my own leadership approach via a mix of professional reading, mentoring and experience via people watching. I must admit it's the latter which has probably been the most powerful and helpful. Watching and learning from others has had a major impact on my approach to leadership in so many ways. I have equally learnt what not to do as well as attempted to replicate leadership actions I have observed others successfully implement."

Here is his list of critical factors that promote successful school leadership.

1. Care about your people.

Providing and promoting a positive work environment is a major influencer on school culture that supports positive school development. A healthy workplace is a happy and productive workplace.

2. Do not micromanage staff.

Professional trust is a foundation for organizational success. Staff that feel valued, empowered, trusted, and appreciated perform better. Provide the conditions for people to lead, support them to succeed, get out of their way, and watch them thrive.

3. Leadership is about developing more leaders.

Leading from the front as well as the side is an effective way to promote leadership skills within others. Leveraging the expertise of staff and allowing authentic opportunities for others to lead is a recipe for success.

4. Be an active learner.

He is always surprised when he sees whole school professional learning workshops in action and the principal is not there. Being present as a learner is very important. Taking learning seriously alongside teachers means that you can be an active participant in driving improved classroom practice. The notion of just "do as I say" just doesn't cut it.

5. Stay humble.

Don't allow positional power to go to your head. Find opportunities to praise the work and effort of others and don't take credit for their work. You can achieve nothing alone.

6. Pick the right team.

That doesn't mean pick those who will just agree with you or do as you say. In fact, having staff who challenge your thinking, operate differently, and have personality traits that aren't the same as yours can provide for a rich staffing mix that avoids artificial harmony.

Borton further explains, "It is always a privilege to lead a school in partnership with its community. Never miss the opportunity to be the best leader you can be. Being the principal of a school is by far and away the best job in the world. Doing it well requires an open mind, ability to adapt and learning new and better ways of operating. Above all be yourself, and don't take yourself too seriously."

One thing that I especially like about Borton is that he keeps it REEL (Richardson Engaging Effective Learners) when it comes to learning. Borton and his team realize that true learning is one that engages the student in meaningful and productive ways. His school is driven by five statements:

1. Students can explain what they are learning and why.

2. Teachers identify the needs of every student.

3. Feedback is given to move learning forward.

4. Students work cooperatively to support each other.

5. Students are responsible for their own learning.

Whether your students are in elementary or secondary education, the REEL principles should be at the core of what you do.

A LEAD LEARNER

Lead learner may be a term that you know regarding school leaders. but it's much more than a title—it's a framework for leadership. When the school leader considers themselves a constant learner, the school system becomes more focused on learning and the people involved see their mission as being a learner as their primary goal. Being a learner allows for risks, failure, investigation, inquiry, feedback, reflection, and discovery. More importantly, a lead learner focuses the school organization, resources, and people toward a centered mindset on the importance of learning. Learning is at the core of everything they do and it's the lens from which everything is filtered.

The responsibility of lead learners is to work collaboratively to nurture a learning culture that is caring, personalized, and results oriented. In regard to caring, school leaders need to create school cultures that make kids want to run to school, not away from it. This is established by connecting every student with a caring adult who believes in them and by providing students the opportunities to get connected and contribute to the school community. We focus on being a lead learner because there should be several lead learners in a school. When school leaders see themselves as the only lead learner, they narrow the learning community and hinder the leadership of their teachers. By using the terms a lead learner or lead learners, it opens up the opportunity for other educators in the building to consider them part of the Lead Learning Team.

One of the most difficult things for school leaders to examine is results-oriented leadership. We hear so much about accountability, but a results orientation is so much more than accountability. It's working with every teacher, staff member, parent, and student to ensure each student is getting positive results in their learning trajectory. These results could be job skills, life skills, relational skills, academic skills, problem solving and critical thinking skills, and organizational skills to compete in the global market. The days of our students only competing for jobs against their hometown rivals is outta here, expired, and outdated. We need to be results-oriented leaders focused on growth, progress, and moving students forward to become active contributors in our global society.

DO WHAT MATTERS

I was privileged to attend a small conference with Dennis Sparks, emeritus director of the National Staff Development Council. He assured the group of leaders that "Anything worth doing is worth doing poorly at first." Leaders don't have to devise a perfect solution before we begin to lead our school. Sparks's words remind us that sustaining leadership takes time, energy, effort, and persistence. He also acknowledges failure as part of the process. Since success requires so much time, energy, resources, and persistence, it's important to spend that effort on things that really matter for your students, staff, and community.

It's okay to start without a perfect plan, but how can a leader continue to learn, and extend learning, throughout their life? How can we make a positive difference for our school and community? John Kotter (1996) offers five key mental habits that support lifelong learning: risk taking, humble self-reflection, solicitation of opinions, careful listening, and openness to new ideas. These areas supply a good focus for our daily work, our routines, and our mindset for continued growth.

RESIST THE QUICK FIX

As a young school leader, I would quickly jump to add the latest thing that I learned through an article, conference, or conversation into my school. I ran through these trendy ideas with great vigor and passion, only to find that the implementation was failed and the buy-in from staff was lost. With social media, it's easier than ever to be constantly chasing after the latest gadget, quick fix, or brilliant idea to implement in your school. However, true system improvement that fosters collaboration and support from faculty and staff does not come in the packaging of these trendy ideas. School leaders need to chase learning, not technology, or the latest quick fix, trendy idea, or popular innovation. Focus on the learning, delve into what strengthens learning, and become an expert on what good learning looks like, sounds like, and feels like. There is nothing wrong with being on the cutting edge of technology or the latest practices in education, but make sure you filter these cutting-edge strategies through the lens of learning.

We can learn from how bank tellers are trained to spot counterfeit money. Rather than learning all the counterfeits out there, and what they feel like, they simply learn and practice with real currency. After working time and time again with real currency, they can instantly detect a phony. The same is true with learning: When we immerse ourselves with what strong learning is, we will know instantly when we see something that is only a passing quick fix or trendy idea.

This is the approach Elliot Eisner (1998) takes when he encourages educational leaders to become connoisseurs of education and learning. Instead of holding up a checklist and seeing what's missing in a classroom, Eisner recommends a school leader should dive deep into the practices of instruction and learning. As we become more and more saturated in quality learning, we can engage in powerful conversations that have the capacity to transform our collective practice and move our schools forward. Ultimately, the school leader will create a space where our students rise to success.

Remember the discussion earlier in the book about "staying a little longer" to boost creativity? This same principle applies here. One of the best ways to resist the pull to "do something right away" is to look for the better solution by slowing down and asking a few questions. The Right Question Institute (http://rightquestion.org) suggests a three-prong approach to questioning. They suggest you start with "Why," moving to "What if," and moving to "How," which can help a solution emerge that is either a substantial revision of the first impulse or a new direction entirely.

Protect Against Distractions

One resource we all have a limited amount of is time. I'm not talking about the number of school days we have compared to Singapore, or how many instructional minutes we lose completing high-stakes testing. Wise school leaders protect their students and staff from distractions to maximize the focus on learning. We believe every school leader starts out with the mission to focus on learning, at least we hope that to be the case. However, we know firsthand that mission to focus on learning can easily go out the window when an angry parent arrives, a student gets injured in gym, there's a problem in the lunchroom, students eat berries from a bush at recess, the police are calling for an investigation, or the fire alarm just went off unexpectedly. Distractions are part of what we experience as school leaders, but they don't need to consume us when it comes to our focus on learning. Make a commitment today to put learning at the forefront.

Below are some strategies that we have found helpful to fight off distractions and prevent them from pulling us away from the core of learning:

- Schedule Time to Be in Classrooms: Block out a part of your day to be in classrooms. Do complete walkthroughs, observations, or just simply visit classes. Schedule part of your day to get into classes, and prevent being distracted and pulled away from this most important work.
- Set Parameters: Let your administrative assistant know that you are out visiting classrooms and to only interrupt you in the event of an emergency.

- Professional Dialogue: If you work with another building leader(s), spend some time walking through classes together so you can reflect on what you saw and extend your professional dialogue. We found this interaction and learning so powerful as we grow our own instructional leadership capacity. Plus, it gets us talking about learning on a regular basis.

- Do E-mail Second: If you arrive early enough to be "alone," getting a jump on e-mail is fine, but instead of allowing your first actions to become lost in the stream of e-mail urgency, make it a point to greet students and staff as they arrive. Take 20 minutes to visit some classrooms informally, and then use the phone or laptop to handle e-mail correspondence. This strategy is a tangible reminder that the tyranny of the urgent does not need to interrupt the things that are most important. Commit to building, and sustaining, quality relationships with students and staff every day. Use e-mail work time as time to be visible. Work in the hallway, the back of a classroom, or the lunchroom. Basically, get out of your office and focus on being around students and staff. This will go a long way in building confidence in you as a leader and in making personal connections.

- Learning Conversations: It's just as important to schedule learning conversations as it is time to be visible and to walk through classrooms. Schedule time to talk with teachers about learning and what they are doing to increase learning in their lessons. Allow for reflective thought from the teacher and use this to examine areas of strengths, improvements, and growth. Reflective listening is so important as a leader; take time to listen, reflect, and allow the teacher to self-assess and reflect on their own practice. Not every conversation needs to be evaluative. We find much growth comes from learning conversations when evaluation is not a part of them. Practice some of the skills in Chapter 1.

- Delegate: There are no superheroes; be sure to delegate the work to teacher leaders, support staff, and fellow school leaders. If you are the only school leader in the building, rely heavily on key teacher leaders to develop leadership capacity. See if the teacher leader would be willing to partner with you to allow you to get freed up to be in classrooms.

KEYS TO LEARNING AS SCHOOL LEADERS

Once you take care of the distractions and the pitfalls of falling into the latest trends, it's important to dig into learning. As a school leader, there is no higher calling than to make sure our students are engaged in relevant, safe, and personalized learning. We need to commit to be leaders who will sacrifice other things to make learning the priority. To do this work, school leaders need to focus on the student, protect learning, get involved, and celebrate the learning.

Focus on Students

Read your latest walkthrough or observation notes. How many times is the teacher's name mentioned compared to students? Most often school leaders focus on the teacher rather than the student. For example, it's common to say things such as "Mrs. Jones started off the lesson with a strong introduction and review of the week ahead. She continued to discuss what today's lesson would include." This phrase never mentions the students and what they are doing. When you are observing a class, conducting a walkthrough, or simply visiting a class, focus on what the students are doing. We need to move our focus away from the teacher and more toward the students. It's about whether the students are learning more than it is if the teacher is performing. Students need to be the ones performing at high levels, and this often parlays into a strong instructional leader teaching the class. This student-centered approach has an added benefit too: When we focus on the students the reflective conversation is stronger because it is more directed to the learning.

Protect Learning

Sadly, learning is disrupted constantly throughout the day by announcements for the custodian, an all-call request, or a particular student to report to the office. Whatever the distractions are, it's our responsibility as school leaders to protect learning and to keep it free from distractions. We understand that some interruptions are unavoidable, but we need to maintain our focus to reduce distractions and protect the learning time.

Get Involved in the Learning

One of our favorite things to do as school leaders is to get involved in the learning. We thrive on joining that chem lab, math lesson, singing in a choral class, or drawing alongside students in art. We need to learn together—that's right, teachers, students, and school leaders learning together in the same classroom. When this happens, students and teachers see you value learning and you are a constant learner. Ask a teacher if you can co-teach a class with them. Join with a teacher and students to teach a lesson. It's about learning together!

We applaud the work of our friend and colleague, Dr. Neil Gupta, who taught us about Shadow a Student. Dr. Gupta is a huge proponent for this most important opportunity to learn and shadow a student because he sees value in learning alongside students and using this time to build relationships with students. The #ShadowAStudent website shared, "This is the process of following a student to gain empathy and insight into their experience." This is a perfect time to learn alongside a student, see what they are learning, and to showcase their work. Join in the Shadow a Student movement and share your work by using the hashtag #ShadowAStudent. Check out the website at www.shadowastudent.org for some tools to get the most of your Shadow a Student experience.

CELEBRATE LEARNING

As school leaders, we celebrate team victories, concert performances, and the latest inventions from our students. Let's take that same vigor into celebrating the numerous learning experiences throughout each school day. Celebrate the learning successes of all students, not just the top prize winners. What we mean here is to showcase all artwork, not just the exemplars that will someday make it to the art museum. Each student's work is important and deserves to be celebrated. Feature learning on your school's social media, post student work throughout the building, and find ways to infuse student work into the community. Many businesses, community organizations, and religious institutions are interested in showcasing student work. Send student writing samples to the local media for publishing, publish your own school's online book, and feature student work in your newsletters and communications. We would like to feature the learning that is going on in your school. Visit our website and share with us the incredible learning that is taking place in your school. What we celebrate grows, so celebrate learning!

Model Learning With Technology

Make sure the methods and approaches you use to promote ongoing professional learning are recursive. Recursive is a great term that computer programmers use, but it's most powerful for us as a visual image—that image is a fern. If you picture a bed of ferns growing in a forest, you can probably envision the triangle-shaped plant nestled next to many others just like it. This image is about repetition, or consistency. Recursive goes a little deeper.

One fern may look just like the fern next to it, but closer inspection of any single plant will show that the "fern shape" you see from 50 feet away actually repeats throughout every level of the plant itself. The fern shape occurs because each leaf has a fern shape, each small part that forms the leaf has the same fern shape, and so on. As a school leader invested in the power of technology for learning, we see an important principle at work here. Each time you engage your staff with ongoing learning it must contain the same elements of technology for learning that you hope to promote in each individual learning community and classroom throughout the school.

Your school will take on a "technology shape" when it becomes the way learning is supported, and extended in all parts of the organization. It's up to the digital leader to ensure the promise of technology for learning never gets isolated to a few superstars, or a few areas of application. Technology has to become the way to teach students what we don't know—a new way to engage in learning, problem solving, and design that has a global audience. To bring this aspiration to reality we must lead with purpose and intentionality, using technology tools to show the way forward from where we are to where we can be.

Let your staff know when you find a new way to learn and hone your leadership practices. Share a great personal learning network resource— not only to share the learning, but to demonstrate how you are learning as a leader. One powerful way to demonstrate the use of technology for learning might be to share how you're learning something outside of school. I can recall a great conversation with a faculty member about my discovery of Scott's Bass Lessons, an online resource that is a tremendous help for any bass player. They see I am learning with technology—professionally and personally.

"Questionstorming" for Better Solutions

You've probably experienced a brainstorming session that resulted in limited storms (or perhaps limited brains), therefore yielding little inspiration, innovation, or direction for moving forward. Some corporations, think tanks, and start-ups are abandoning brainstorming and replacing it with "questionstorming." This not-so-subtle shift recognizes that the quest for more and more answers often paralyzes the process and engagement of your group, while questions often build an energy and excitement that invigorates a group (Berger, 2014).

School Leader's Story
Changing a School Culture for Learning

Photo courtesy of Ryan Maxwell

Leader: Ryan Maxwell

School: Sunnyside High School

Website: http://www.sunnysideschools
.org/Domain/8

Setting: Suburban

Size: 1,900 students (800 student
increase in four years)

Grades: 9–12

Population: 91% Hispanic, 9% white

Poverty: 100% economically disadvantaged

District: Sunnyside School District

State: Sunnyside, WA

We close this book with an example of transformational learning and leadership that has taken Sunnyside High School from one of the bottom 5% of high schools in the state of Washington, to one of the top 5% high schools in a six-year time span. School leader Ryan Maxwell (2016 Washington Principal of the Year) and his team of teachers, students, and parents raised the graduation rate from 46% to 90%. Maxwell shares, "We have gone from a school with massive gang issues where three 12th-grade students died of gang violence in one year, to a school that has a positive and caring culture." Sunnyside High School, located in the heart of apple orchard country, thoughtfully implemented a one-to-one initiative with Chromebooks. The school's website shares, "The 1:1 Technology Initiative is directly tied to the Sunnyside School District's goal that all students will have the technological skills to be successful at college and career levels. We believe access to digital devices at school and at home will allow learning to continue in this technology-rich and globally connected world." In addition, the school dramatically increased dual-enrollment opportunities for students, having many of their students graduate from high school with an associate degree. Students leave Sunnyside High with the skills to be successful in college, career, and beyond.

The *Daily Sun* reported at Ryan's principal award ceremony. Maxwell was nominated for the honor by Heidi Hellner-Gomez, the district's

(Continued)

(Continued)

executive director of instructional leadership. "I nominated him because he is a leader not only in our district, but in the region and the state, in high school reform. He has led in a creative and fearless way that has bettered education for high school students and the students of Sunnyside School District."

Maxwell and his team believe this has been accomplished by their common vision of 100% graduation. He goes on to share, "Through an equal focus on relational trust, social support, and academic press with staff and students, we have created nearly infallible systems that have led to a culture of success."

Maxwell's leadership showcases the influence school leaders have on their school, community, and state. He's become a local, state, and national leader on high school reform. Sunnyside's success is the result of future focused leaders who have a tireless, fearless, creative, and strategic commitment to success for every student.

Key Chapter Takeaways

Leading and lifelong learning go hand in hand. A mindset that supports the belief that we can get smarter, more creative, and more influential in our leadership underpins successful leadership work. Our leadership learning happens in a social context, too. That's one of the reasons it's so important to mentor younger leaders and hear from established leaders—we all learn together when we bring a rich collection of experiences together to analyze, dissect, reflect on, and apply to our own leadership practice. Be sure to spend time in classrooms to not just observe and critique, but to engage with, and learn with, your teachers and students. Consider taking/teaching a course in your community education program, area college, local YMCA, or senior center. It's valuable to become a student again.

RELATE, INNOVATE, INVIGORATE ACTIVITIES

Relate

- Get Into Classrooms – Visit at least three classrooms every day.
- Join in on the Learning – Be a participant and learn alongside of teachers and students.
- Learning Conversations – Be sure to focus conversations around the learning. Hold a learning conversation today.

Innovate

- Lead Learner – Be sure to have a mindset of learning and consider yourself a lead learner for the school.
- Questionstorm – Host a questionstorming session with staff and students.
- Shadow a Student – Join in on the #ShadowAStudent and learn about what it's like to be a student for the day.

Invigorate

- Protect Learning – This may sound odd, but by protecting what we value most, teachers and students are energized and see the importance of learning. Review your public announcements protocol, reduce interruptions in the building, and keep learning at the center of all you do.
- Spread the Word – Publish a story that highlights a teacher using technology well to extend learning, including examples of student-created work. Be sure to share these with us as we would like to feature your school on our website.
- Host a Conference – Host a school leaders conference at your building to share ideas to avoid the "quick fix" solutions being used in so many systems. Identify a person to capture the event via video (or live stream) so the dialogue can be shared with other leaders.

Team Talk

Team Talk Stories is a conversation space for school leadership teams to share their stories from experiences with the Team Talk activities at the end of each chapter; visit **www.chaselearning.org/TeamTalk**.

Our final Team Talk activity may be the best of them all (your team will have to determine that ranking). We encourage you to plan with your leadership team for two events: to host another school's leadership team and to travel to an "away game" with a school who is willing to do the same. If we can all get smarter, more creative, and better at our leadership work, then we can certainly benefit from gathering as leaders. While a conference, PLN, or the web resources at Chase Learning can supply some powerful learning opportunities, we're hoping this "home/away" meeting event can help your team establish a relationship with other leaders who are nearby. It may even produce a pooling of resources to help an extended community of folks.

Remember to explore more resources—including links for all the URLs listed in the book, organized by chapter—online at **www.chaselearning .org**.

Thanks for reading *Future Focused Leaders*. It's been a privilege to start the conversation with you, and we look forward to many other opportunities to connect and learn from each other. Press on in the work.

Bill and Dave

Continue the conversation with us on Twitter at #chaselearning.

Appendix

SwERI Digital Leadership Rubric

		Description	Relate Example	Innovate Example	Invigorate Example
Sw	**Switch**	Technology does not change the leadership process or product; it simply switches from analog to digital.	Leader replaces e-mail with texting communication for staff and community.	Leader replaces desktop or laptop computer with notebooks, but tasks remain relatively unchanged.	Leader replaces student on the bulletin board with social media solution to highlight role models from the student body.
E	**Extend**	Technology adds value or capability to the leadership process or product that was not available before.	Leader uses a blog to promote dialogue to flow in both directions, allowing professional staff and community member to respond.	Leader obtains discounted packages or portable hotpots to allow disadvantaged families to gain Internet access at home.	Leader uses stories of schools that changed learning with technology at faculty meetings and community events.
R	**Realize**	Technology applied to an authentic leadership problem, process, or product within or beyond the school system.	Leader creates digital stories to highlight teacher success and shares with professional staff and community.	Leader uses cloud-based solutions to gather informal walkthrough data and share with staff to examine collective practices at the school.	Leader gathers survey data for identified problem through a web-based form, allowing students and community members to weigh in.
I	**Innovate**	Technology used to create a leadership process, product, or solution that would not be possible without the integration of technology.	Leader uses desktop video to gather collaborators beyond the school system for professional learning for themselves and their staff.	Leader creates a mobile data collection system that finds a community problem for students to solve.	Leader works with community partners to repurpose a physical space for entrepreneurship opportunities with community businesses.

References

Berger, W. (2014). *A more beautiful question: The power of inquiry to spark break-through ideas*. New York, NY: Bloomsbury.

Boaler, J. (2016). *Mathematical mindsets: Unleashing students' potential through creative math, inspiring messages, and innovative teaching*. San Francisco, CA: Jossey-Bass.

deBono, E. (1999). *Six thinking hats*. New York, NY: Little, Brown and Company.

DoSomething.org. (n.d.). 11 facts about high school dropout rates. Available at https://www.dosomething.org/us/facts/11-facts-about-high-school-drop out-rates

Double the Donation. (2016). Available at https://doublethedonation.com/com panies-that-donate-to-nonprofits/

Dweck, C. S. (2016). *Mindset: The new psychology of success*. New York, NY: Penguin Random House.

Eisner, E. W. (1998). *The enlightened eye: Qualitative inquiry and the enchantment of educational practice*. Upper Saddle River, NJ: Prentice Hall.

Farrell, S. (2016, July 21). Facebook's solar-powered internet plane takes flight. *The Guardian*. Available at https://www.theguardian.com/business/2016/jul/21/facebook-solar-powered-internet-plane-test-flight-aquila

Federal Interagency Forum on Child and Family Statistics. (2011). *America's chil-dren: Key national indicators of well-being 2011*. Washington, DC: Government Printing Office. Accessed at www.childstats.gov/pdf/ac2011/ac_11.pdf

Follows, S. (2014, February 24). How many people work on a Hollywood film? [Blog post]. Retrieved from https://stephenfollows.com/how-many-people-work-on-a-hollywood-film/

Fullan, M., Hill, P., & Crévola, C. (2006). *Breakthrough*. Thousand Oaks, CA: Corwin.

Ginsburg, K. (2015). *Raising kids to thrive: Balancing love with expectations and pro-tection with trust*. Elk Grove Village, IL: American Academy of Pediatricians.

Jensen, E. (2016). *Poor students, rich teaching: Mindsets for change*. Bloomington, IL: Solution Tree Press.

Jorgensen, R., & Hurst, D. (2009). *Oracle of the obvious: Secrets of common sense leadership*. Landrum, SC: JLC Publishing.

Kotter, J. P. (1996). *Leading change*. Boston, MA: Harvard Business Review Press.

Lazarus, E. (1883). The new colossus. *Emma Lazarus: Selected poems and other writings.* Retrieved from https://www.poetryfoundation.org/poems-and-poets/poems/detail/46550

Michelli, J. A. (2007). *The Starbucks experience: Five principles for turning ordinary into extraordinary.* New York, NY: McGraw-Hill.

Morgridge Center for Public Service. (2014, December 8). *Life behind bars: Children with an incarcerated parent.* University of Wisconsin–Madison. Accessed May 31, 2016, at http://dept.camden.rutgers.edu/nrccfi/files/Factsheet7-Incarceration.pdf

National Center for Educational Statistics. (2014a). Elementary and secondary schools: Enrollment by race and ethnicity. https://nces.ed.gov/programs/digest/mobile/Enrollment_ES_Enrollment_by_Race_and_Ethnicity.aspx

National Center for Educational Statistics. (2014b). Enrollment: Elementary and secondary schools. https://nces.ed.gov/programs/digest/mobile/Enrollment_ES.aspx

National Center for Educational Statistics (2016, December). Digest of education statistics: 2015. https://nces.ed.gov/programs/digest/d15/

November, A., (2010). *Empowering students with technology* (2nd ed.). Thousand Oaks, CA: Corwin.

Ramage, D. (2007). *Digital stories for professional learning: Reflection and technology integration in the classroom.* Ann Arbor: University of Michigan Press.

Robinson, K. (2011). *Out of our minds: Learning to be creative.* Chichester, United Kingdom: Capstone Publishing.

Sawchuk, S. (2014). Steep drop seen in teacher-prep enrollment numbers. *Education Week.* Accessed June 1, 2016, at http://www.edweek.org/ew/articles/2014/10/22/09enroll.h34.html

Senge, P. M. (2006). *The fifth discipline: The art and practice of the learning organization.* New York, NY: Doubleday.

Sparks, S. D. (2015). Children of inmates seen at risk. *Education Week.* Accessed May 31, 2016, at http://www.edweek.org/ew/articles/2015/02/25/parents-incarceration-takes-toll-on-children-studies.html

STEM Education Foundation. (n.d.). Shenzhen, China. Retrieved from http://en.chinastem.org/index.html

Sydell, L. (2017, January 9). Can virtual reality make you more empathetic? In NPR (Producer), *All Things Considered.* Retrieved from http://www.npr.org/sections/alltechconsidered/2017/01/09/508617333/can-virtual-reality-make-you-more-empathetic

Tarte, J. (2015, July 22). Student partnership in professional development. Edutopia. Retrieved from http://www.edutopia.org/blog/student-partnership-in-professional-development-justin-tarte

The Right Question Institute. (n.d.). Available at http://rightquestion.org

Torrance, E. P. (1995). *Why fly?: A philosophy of creativity (creativity research).* Westport, CT: Praeger. ISBN 978-1567501735

Wheatley, M. J. (1994). *Leadership and the new science.* San Francisco, CA: Berret-Kohler.

Wojcick, S. (2011). *The eight pillars of innovation.* Available at https://www.think withgoogle.com/articles/8-pillars-of-innovation.html

World Economic Forum. (2016). *Future of jobs report: Employment, skills and workforce strategy for the fourth industrial revolution.* Available at http://www3 .weforum.org/docs/WEF_Future_of_Jobs.pdf

Ziegler, W. (2005). *A case study on the Pottstown school district's school safety program: A proactive approach to school safety for principals.* Ann Arbor: University of Michigan Press.

Ziegler, W., & Ramage, D. (2012, April). Taking a risk: Sharing leadership and power. *Principal Leadership, 12*(8), 34–38.

Index

A SAGE Publishing Company

CORWIN HAS ONE MISSION: to enhance education through intentional professional learning.

We build long-term relationships with our authors, educators, clients, and associations who partner with us to develop and continuously improve the best evidence-based practices that establish and support lifelong learning.

Solutions you want. Experts you trust.
Results you need.